Y0-CBL-973

MEASURING THE SOFTWARE PROCESS

A Practical Guide to Functional Measurements

Selected Titles from the
YOURDON PRESS COMPUTING SERIES
Ed Yourdon, *Advisor*

ANDREWS AND LEVENTHAL Fusion: Integrating IE, CASE, and JAD
ANDREWS AND STALICK Business Reenigineering: The Survival Guide
AUGUST Joint Application Design
BODDIE The Information Asset: Rational DP Funding and Other Radical Notions
BOULDIN Agents of Change: Managing the Introduction of Automated Tools
BRILL Building Controls into Structured Systems
COAD AND NICOLA Object-Oriented Programming
COAD AND YOURDON Object-Oriented Analysis, 2/E
COAD AND YOURDON Object-Oriented Design
COAD WITH NORTH AND MAYFIELD Object Models: Strategies, Patterns, and Applications
CONNELL AND SHAFER Object-Oriented Rapid Prototyping
CONNELL AND SHAFER Structured Rapid Prototyping
CONSTANTINE Constantine on Peopleware
CONSTANTINE AND YOURDON Structured Design
CRAWFORD Advancing Business Concepts in a JAD Workshop Setting
DeGRACE AND STAHL The Olduvai Imperative: CASE and the State of Software Engineering
      Practice
DeGRACE AND STAHL Wicked Problems, Righteous Solutions
DeMARCO Controlling Software Projects
DeMARCO Structured Analysis and System Specification
EMBLEY, KURTZ, AND WOODFIELD Object-Oriented Systems Analysis
FOURNIER Practical Guide to Structured System Development and Maintenance
GARMUS AND HERRON Measuring the Software Process
GLASS Software Conflict: Essays on the Art and Science of Software Engineering
JONES Assessment and Control of Software Risks
KING Project Management Made Simple
LARSON Interactive Software: Tools for Building Interactive User Interfaces
McMENAMIN AND PALMER Essential System Design
MOSLEY The Handbook of MIS Application Software Testing
PAGE-JONES Practical Guide to Structured Systems Design, 2/E
PINSON Designing Screen Interfaces in C
PUTNAM AND MYERS Measures for Excellence: Reliable Software on Time within Budget
RIPPS An Implementation Guide to Real-Time Programming
RODGERS ORACLE®: A Database Developer's Guide
RODGERS UNIX®: Database Management Systems
SHLAER AND MELLOR Object Lifecycles: Modeling the World in States
SHLAER AND MELLOR Object-Oriented Systems Analysis: Modeling the World in Data
THOMSETT Third Wave Project Management
WANG (ed.) Information Technology in Action
WARD System Development Without Pain
WARD AND MELLOR Structured Development for Real-Time Systems
YOURDON Decline and Fall of the American Programmer
YOURDON Managing the Structured Techniques, 4/E
YOURDON Managing the System Life-Cycle, 2/E
YOURDON Modern Structured Analysis
YOURDON Object-Oriented Systems Design
YOURDON Structured Walkthroughs, 4/E
YOURDON Techniques of Program Structure and Design
YOURDON, WHITEHEAD, THOMANN, OPPEL, AND NEVERMANN Mainstream Objects: An
      Analysis and Design Approach for Business
YOURDON INC. YOURDON™ Systems Method: Model-Driven Systems Development

MEASURING THE SOFTWARE PROCESS

A Practical Guide to Functional Measurements

David Garmus
and
David Herron

For book and bookstore information

http://www.prenhall.com

YOURDON PRESS
Prentice Hall PTR
Upper Saddle River, New Jersey 07458

Library of Congress Cataloging–in–Publication Data

Garmus, David.
    Managing the software process : a practical guide to functional
    measurements / David Garmus and David Herron.
        p.   cm.
    Includes bibliographical references and index.
    ISBN 0–13–349002–5
    1. Computer software—Development   Management.   I. Herron, David
P. II. Title.
QA76.76.D47G37   1996
005.1′4—dc20   95–41170
                                                                        CIP

Acquisitions editor: Paul Becker
Cover designer: Talar Agasyan
Cover design director: Jerry Votta
Manufacturing buyer: Alexis R. Heydt
Compositor/Production services: Pine Tree Composition, Inc.

 Published by Prentice Hall PTR
Prentice-Hall, Inc.
A Simon & Schuster Company
Upper Saddle River, New Jersey 07458

The publisher offers discounts on this book when ordered in
bulk quantities.

For more information contact:
  Corporate Sales Department
  Prentice Hall PTR
  One Lake Street
  Upper Saddle River, New Jersey 07458

  Phone: 800–382–3419
  Fax: 201–236–7141
  email: corpsales@prenhall.com

Printed in the United States of America
10 9 8 7 6 5 4 3 2 1

ISBN: 0-13-349002-5

Prentice Hall International (UK) Limited, *London*
Prentice Hall of Australia Pty. Limited, *Sydney*
Prentice Hall Canada, Inc., *Toronto*
Prentice Hall Hispanoamericana, S.A., *Mexico*
Prentice Hall of India Private Limited, *New Delhi*
Prentice Hall of Japan, Inc., *Tokyo*
Simon & Schuster Asia Pte. Ltd., *Sinapore*
Editora Prentice Hall do Brasil, Ltda., *Rio de Janeiro*

CONTENTS

ACKNOWLEDGMENTS

A book represents much more than the result of taking pen to paper. In our case this book represents our professional experiences. Those experiences shaped our lives, thoughts, and opinions, many of which are reflected herein. The foundation of those experiences was our interaction with a large number of people. Consequently, this book is really the result of many contributions, from many individuals over the years. We would like to acknowledge each of those individuals and thank them for their support. We don't have enough pages to include many of you who have had a positive impact on us, but we both appreciate the thoughts and ideas which you have shared with us and hope that you will continue to do so in the future. This is particularly true for those of you involved with software measurement, especially the membership of the International Function Point Users Group (IFPUG) and its foreign affiliates.

We deeply appreciate the love, support, and patience from our wives, Caren Way Garmus and Mary Roswell Herron, while we wrote this book and on a daily basis while we spent far too many hours on the road and working while we were at home. We are also thankful for their many ideas and contributions to the success of our business, The David Consulting Group.

We are particularly grateful for the relationships we have shared with other leaders in the software measurement profession, including Allan Albrecht, Charlie

Gold, Dave Gelperin, Bill Hetzel, Capers Jones, Chris Kemerer, Larry Meador, and Larry Putnam.

The very knowledgeable reviewers of this book have our everlasting gratitude and should be credited with part ownership. We incorporated most of their suggestions which resulted in a better product. Thanks to Allan Albrecht, the inventor of Function Points, and Frank Mazzucco, the current IFPUG President and another longtime friend.

Some of our friends and associates were generous enough to contribute directly to this book. Their firsthand experiences in software measurement will be appreciated and enjoyed by many readers. Our thanks to Dr. Sam Bayer of Sapiens, Ken Florian of RDI Software Technologies, Randy Fraysher of AT&T Global Information Solutions and Paul Lusher of the Naval Surface Warfare Center, US Navy.

There have been many other professional contacts who have supported our causes and influenced our minds. They especially include Mary Bradley, Patrick Cusack, Jacqueline Jones, Cheryl Lampshire, Alex Lubashevsky and Linda Smith and many others including Alain Abran, Ross Barrington, Dan Bradley, Don Buchanan, Larry Campbell, Al Coblentz, Larry Classen, Dawn Coley, Stan Cutler, Carol Dekkers, Jean-Marc Desharnais, Rich Desjardins, Rob Donnellan, Gail Flaherty, Barbara Gardner, Steve Galea, Stuart Glickman, Jim Glorie, Paul Goodman, Mike Goodrich, Brian Handley, Fred Herczeg, Bill Hittel, Robert Krahl, Alan Kusinitz, Paula Jamieson, Francesca Lesnoni, Mark Mandel, Jean Melancon, Giovanni Modica, Lloyd Mosemann, Domenico Natale, Jolijn Onvlee, Nadine Printsky, Robin Ragland, Eberhard Rudolph, Grant Rule, Bill Rumpf, Denis St-Pierre, Adri Timp, Eddy van Vliet, Gary Walker, Scott Whitmire and Eli Williamson.

Perhaps most important of all have been clients and friends, some of whom have included Jeff Holman and Jeanne Horner of AT&T; Jeanne Carlisle, Steve Fugale and Carolyn Szalkowski of Cigna; Tom Kirchgessner of CPI; Paul Beamish, Wayne Condra, John King and Lisa Mc Daniels of Delta; Sheila Dennis and Kathy Watson of DFAS; Sharon Hill-Weidman and many others of DuPont; Ellen Heidkamp and Wayne Ratz of General Accident; Janae Daley of Hill AFB; Michael Cheung of IBAX; Rich Prestera of ISSC Eckerd; Jeff Gruver and Don Walker of ISSC Hertz; David Pauls, Chris Faiferlick, Charles Tichenor and Steve Wilson of the IRS; Tony Williams of Sprint; and Robert Fahey and Terry Vogt of TransQuest.

We thank the staff of the IFPUG Office, particularly Betty Westbrook but also Kathy Chapman Egolf, Gloria Crase and Rachael Pepper, for their continuing support.

Finally we thank and dedicate this book to our parents and children. First to our parents (Paul & Mary Garmus and Earl & Mildred "Buddy" Herron) and our wives' parents (William & Wanda Roswell and Charles and Lila Way) who gave so much of themselves to help and encourage us along the way. Second to our children (Kimberlie, Danelle, Joshua, Jason, Alexander, and Elizabeth) who, we hope, will have success and joy in all their endeavors.

FOREWORD

Allan Albrecht has been known as the inventor of Function Points since the method was first introduced in 1979. We have had the good fortune to work with Allan over many years. He has been gracious enough to share with us and many others his time, knowledge, and insights into this invaluable software measurement technique.

We are indebted to Allan and hope to retain our friendship for many years to come.

The following comments were provided by Allan Albrecht after reading the proof copy of our book:

"Function Points: A Software Metric" will fill a real need for the added clarification, perspective, and illustration of the uses of the Function Points measure. The coverage of the following topics are especially gratifying:

> The Gun Computing System Function Point Count illustrates the effective use of the Function Points measure for Real-Time Control Systems.
>
> The GUI Function Point Example extends Function Points into modern design applications.
>
> The Estimating Chapter clarifies the differences between the functional General Adjustment Factor and the productivity Influencers needed for a complete estimate.

INTRODUCTION

This is a book about Function Points. More to the point, this is a book about how to successfully execute the Function Point counting methodology. Function Point counting is one of the fastest growing software management techniques in the software industry today. It is used by a variety of organizations across numerous industry types. To some, the Function Point methodology is the cornerstone of their software development and management. To others, it is simply one of many software management tools that are used to successfully build systems.

To understand the specific and practical application of the Function Point methodology, it is necessary to consider the full scope of software measurement and software management. The first two chapters of this book present a general overview of software measurement and provide the context in which the Function Point methodology should be presented. From there the book devotes numerous chapters to the specific rules and guidelines of the Function Point methodology. Finally, the book concludes with discussions and examples of Function Point uses and benefits.

This book is designed to serve primarily as a reference guide and to be used to educate the reader on Function Point counting techniques. The book defines the current rules and guidelines set forth by the International Function Point Users Group (IFPUG). The book also makes use of practical and detailed counting examples to provide the reader with a clear understanding of how to apply the Function Point counting technique.

Since its inception, the Function Point methodology has been enhanced numerous times. Seldom have these enhancements changed the general counting rules, that were initially established. The enhancements are commonly focused on improving the clarity of definitions, rules, and guidelines. The enhancements are also necessary in order to keep pace with the evolution of technology. The Function Point technique is intended to give equivalent results regardless of the application or the technologies used. Thus, it is vital that its definitions and examples accurately and sensitively recognize, highlight, and describe the Function Point components in the different applications and technologies such as Graphical User Interface (GUI) and Object Oriented (OO) environments. The time has come to deliver a new publication on the whys, wherefores, and ways of counting Function Points.

Brian Dreger authored what is considered to be the first practical layman's guide and instruction to Function Point analysis. *Function Point Analysis* was published in the fall of 1989 and was generally accepted as a standard for counting Function Points. This was at a time when the IFPUG organization was just beginning to define itself and its role in the software industry. It was also a time when Function Point activities were mostly limited to those select organizations that had the insight to understand the usefulness of the Function Point method. Such companies as AT&T, Motorola, Hewlett-Packard, and Boeing were among the early users of the methodology. Because of the high profile of these companies, and because of their reputations as quality producers of software, Function Points began to gain exposure to a wider audience. Dreger's book was soon found in many executive offices where there was a continuous search for improved software management techniques.

Over time the need to update Dreger's original work has become obvious. As the IFPUG organization grew in size and prominence, it naturally took on the role as being the keeper of the Function Point guidelines. Early work by the volunteer committees at IFPUG provided critical support for the early versions of the official *Counting Practices Manual*.

Today, there is a well-documented and maintained set of counting guidelines that are available to all IFPUG members. Even with the existence of this official reference guide, there is still a void in the marketplace. Naturally, not everyone is aware of the IFPUG organization, but many have heard of Function Points and desire to learn more about this technique. Beyond the IFPUG guidelines there is a need to present Function Points in a more readable format. It is also critical to put Function Points in their proper perspective. They are not a panacea for all the ills of the software community. Often, instead of describing what Function Points do, consultants find themselves describing what Function Points don't do. This is not the result of any shortcomings in the Function Point counting process itself but more from general misunderstandings that exist in the marketplace today.

This book provides an excellent opportunity for us to expand on the pure technical application of Function Point counting. The IFPUG guidelines are for the Function Point practitioner; so too is this book. In addition to the practice of counting Function Points and the techniques involved, there is also the need to understand the practical uses of Function Points. This book affords us the opportunity to raise the level of awareness of the value of software measurement while at the same time educating the practitioner about the details of Function Points as a software metric.

There is an ever expanding technical audience that is eager to learn about counting Function Points. Some have already formed impressions and attitudes about the capabilities and value of Function Points. These impressions are often erroneous and ill-conceived. It is necessary for all levels in an organization to learn how to properly count and use Function Points.

It is with these goals in mind that we present the material in a logical, educational, and practical manner. First, we address the issue of software measurement and management. After building a case for measurement, and positioning Function Points within that context, we focus on the counting technique itself. Once that technique has been explained, we then move into detailed and practical applications of the technique. A more detailed description of the sections follows.

THE BUSINESS OF SOFTWARE

To begin this book with a detailed and technical discussion about the rules and techniques of the Function Point methodology would be like looking at the trees without considering the whole forest. It would provide you all you need to know about Function Points, but you wouldn't necessarily understand how to use Function Points to manage the overall software development environments. Chapter 1 sets the stage for the Function Point methodology. If we can agree that developing software is more of a business or a process than an art form, then we can also agree that a business or process needs to be managed through the use of various control functions. Function Points are one of these control mechanisms.

MEASURING PERFORMANCE

Chapter 1 focuses our attention on the need to manage our software business. From this vantage point we then need to know what opportunities exist to successfully manage the business of software. In Chapter 2 we discuss the various measurement techniques available. We learn that there are quantitative and qualitative aspects to software measurement. Function Points are classified as one of the key quantitative measures.

THE FUNCTION POINT METHOD

The Function Point methodology is presented in detail in Chapters 3 through 7. In a step-by-step approach, each of the Function Point chapters addresses the tasks necessary to complete accurate Function Point counts. When appropriate, detailed examples are presented, and exercises are provided to enhance the learning experience.

The presented rules and guidelines are aligned with the rules and guidelines recommended by the IFPUG Counting Practices Committee. We recognize the IFPUG *Counting Practices Manual* as the standard and give total credit to IFPUG for the counting rules contained in our book.

This section of the book can be used as an initial training guide and then as a useful reference guide later on. It also provides the foundation for developing enhanced counting practices guidelines which can be supplemented with examples of specific counting situations for an organization.

CASE STUDIES

Chapters 8 and 9 can be considered among the most important of the entire book. We have taken the counting principles and demonstrated, through the use of case studies, how they are applied in a variety of ways. This section also provides the reader an opportunity to better understand the flexibility of this methodology across different environments.

ACCURATE ESTIMATING

The Function Point methodology was born out of the need to find an improved software sizing technique for more accurate estimating. Chapter 10 deals with the application of Function Points in a basic estimating model. The techniques for estimation are not revolutionary or even new. This chapter demonstrates the various ways that Function Points may be used in estimating software projects, whether that estimate is required early in the requirements phase of a project or in the later stages of development for project control.

SUCCESS STORIES

Nothing speaks better of a methodology than examples of its successful application. Chapter 11 presents four success stories from companies with diverse technical environments and varied software measurement needs. We demonstrate first hand how these organizations are using Function Points to successfully manage their software business.

OPPORTUNITY FOR AUTOMATION

There is a definite progression in learning about and implementing this methodology. The first phase is understanding and acceptance. Second is determining how these techniques will be integrated into existing practices. Training of staff is the next step of the progression. Finally, everyone wants to know if they can automate the process. In Chapter 12 you will find a reference guide to automation opportunities.

APPENDIX

This book contains many useful guides, worksheets, and reference lists in its appendixes. Of greatest importance perhaps is the CFPS Practice Exam section. These materials will allow you to test your knowledge of the specific counting guideline, and can serve as a study guide for IFPUG certification.

We sincerely hope that you enjoy this book. We also hope that it will enhance your understanding of Function Points and allow you to use Function Points to improve development practices.

1

THE BUSINESS
OF SOFTWARE

A SOFTWARE BUSINESS MODEL

The planning, designing, building, delivering, and supporting of software has become a critical and integral component of the business world today. Whether a company's primary business is to develop, market, and sell software commercially or to build software systems for internal operational support, the importance of software to the business is felt throughout the organization. Noted software expert Capers Jones suggests that as a profession, software engineers and programmers have increased in number 10% annually over the last thirty years. In some large companies the number of software professionals range into the hundreds and represent as much as 10% to 20% of the company's budget. Budgets to support the internal software business unit have increased dramatically over the last ten years and now command the attention of Chief Executive Officers (CEOs) and Chief Information Officers (CIOs) alike. The significance of these facts is that developing software has become a critical part of our business operation. Unfortunately, the tools and techniques we use to manage the software operation have not reached the level of discipline that we find in other operational units such as finance or human resources. We are now realizing the importance of managing software risks, calculating return on the technology investment, and considering strategic business alignment to Information Technology.

The ability of an organization to effectively and efficiently manage data provides a true competitive advantage and adds value to the company's bottom line. In order for a company to manage the data successfully the Information Systems (IS) organization must properly and effectively manage the development and deployment of those systems that manage data. The problem with today's company is the lack of a basis or benchmark for properly establishing expectations around performance levels, time to market, product performance, and delivery of quality software. There is no standard to measure the software process. As software professionals, we have not fully acknowledged the fact that developing software is a business unto itself that requires unique measures and monitors.

This lack of commitment to the "business" of developing software is readily observed through the organizational ping-pong that has been played with the IS business unit. The issue of where IS should report within the organization resulted in organization charts defining responsibility under Finance, under the CEO, or within the business units. When none of these solutions produced satisfactory results, a new level of professional was invented; the CIO. The software issue is not an organizational one; it's a managerial one. Most business organizations simply do not have an understanding of how to effectively manage their software environments. IS organizations are not often viewed as a unique business function within the organization. They are more often considered a part of something else.

The first and most crucial step to successfully managing the software environment is to consider it as a unique business practice within the organization. This is not a revolutionary idea. In fact, we believe that a company that decides to outsource its software operation has the fundamental understanding that software requires business type management practices. The decision to outsource is based upon the recognition of software management as essential, from a cost perspective, and unique, from a managerial perspective; therefore, some order of professional management is required, different from the other business units. There are basic principles to successful software management that can and must be applied, whether internally managed or outsourced.

The software industry is in a constant state of change. With advances in hardware, software, graphical, and multimedia technologies, applications are constantly being rethought, redesigned, and reengineered. New development methods and techniques are continuously evolving. Because of this environment of continuous change, the software environment or software business can be extremely difficult to manage.

Effective change management techniques require consistent and meaningful measures. This is a book about Function Points, and also, in part, a book about software measurement. In order to understand the added value of Function Points and their use as an effective and dynamic software measure, it is important to put the managing of software in perspective. The perspective we want to take is a business one.

As an example, a manufacturing company follows a business paradigm that involves delivering goods based on customer demand. That paradigm is a well-defined framework that includes sales and marketing, product planning and control, manufacturing, inventory, and accounting. The manufacturing business deals with key business monitors that include market potential, sales forecasts, manufacturing capacity, inventory status, cost of goods, unit cost, product quality, and output per worker.

Similarly, a service company must also deal in a paradigm suited to its need to monitor services delivered based on customer demand. Here too we see a well-defined framework that includes sales, marketing, product development, operational control, customer support, and accounting. The key business monitors involved in service include market potential, market share, sales forecast, and profit margins.

Thinking about software as a unique business function requires acknowledged and accepted standards of practice. It means that there is some measure of business performance and some ability to measure the value of the investment to the bottom line profitability. If we were to view the software development environment as a business unto itself, we would see many of the same elements of manufacturing and service oriented businesses.

The business model presented in Figure 1.1 is familiar to us; one we can comfortably accept. It presents us with a perspective of how to view the software business unit. The issues with which the software "business" must deal are every bit as important as other critical business issues. The key business monitors become cost control, improving time to market, delivering quality software, and perhaps most importantly, realizing added value to the primary business. When we think about software as a unique business function we have to consider its uniqueness with regard to how we will measure performance.

Controlling costs is consistently reported as the number one issue in the soft-

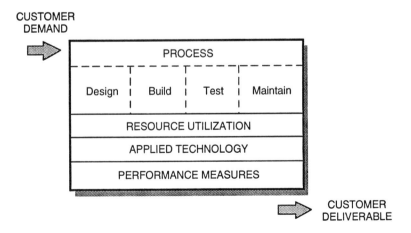

FIGURE 1.1   The Software Business Model

ware development environment. It is no wonder that the increased data processing costs, both in hardware expense and software expense, have finally gained the attention of senior management. Senior executives are demanding to know why, how, and on what they are spending their technology dollars. As money gets tighter budgets get cut, and expenses must be reduced. The focus is constantly on quicker, better, and cheaper software development. Software business units are viewed as just another line item; therefore, much more emphasis is placed on cost reduction. If we were to take the view that the software organization should be run like a business, then both sides of the ledger would be properly balanced. This would suggest that we look at the software entity as a business to achieve profitability.

In essence, this is part of the success and the fascination with outsourcing. Outsourcing demands that the software environment be run like a business. The relationship between the outsourcing provider and the customer is a contractual, business relationship. In the relationship, the product deliverable (software) is initially bid, the price is negotiated and then mutually agreed upon together with the rate of pay and the measures of performance for the end deliverable (see Figure 1.2). Function Points can play a major role in these arrangements.

Time to market is always an issue in a competitive business environment. For as long as software has been developed, managers have always wanted it to be done quicker, with no sense of long-term costs. This approach to software development is negatively viewed and often labeled as "quick and dirty". An entire subindustry of automated support tools called Computer Aided Software Engineering (CASE) was born out of the market demand for quicker deliverables. The need for increased performance is very real as the software industry is a globally competitive business. Businesses need to find a competitive advantage, and they realize that their advantage can be found in timely data. Any company can hire the skills, buy the tools, and develop the marketing team to apply general principles to advance its product. The only real distinguishing feature of an organization is its data. Delivery of that data in an accurate and timely fashion becomes essential to the company's survival.

Finally, and perhaps most importantly, is the notion of *visibility and strategic integration*; for example, the return on the technology investment. The commercial software market fully realizes the importance of demonstrating value to their customers. Increasingly the IS business unit has become more visible to its internal customer. More and more software directors are being required to demonstrate or quantify the value of the IS dollar being spent. Increasing budgets, coupled with

FIGURE 1.2   Software Business Relationship Model

longer time to market issues are not an acceptable combination. Managers must maximize the return on every IS dollar spent.

MANAGING SOFTWARE RISKS

In managing today's business, not only are we concerned with performance, but we are also focused on managing risk. Similarly, in the business of building software, it is important to manage risk. To do this effectively, several key factors must be in place. First, we must posess an overall awareness of the possible risks in managing software. Second, a vehicle must be in place to help identify those risks. Finally, knowledge of strategic business directions should be present in order for a company to properly prioritize opportunities for risk reduction. The key to successful risk management is in the ability to measure.

Certainly the most popular risk management technique involves the deployment of new technologies. The number of computer aided tools and software available on the market today speaks to the demands of the marketplace to find quick answers from a single source. Unfortunately, that is not realistic. It is only through a combination of tools, techniques, and methods that one can improve the overall process and minimize risks.

There are a number of external factors that also play a significant role in our evaluation of risks. Outside influences such as user conflicts, inadequately defined requirements, or changing business commitments all play a vital role.

For an organization to effectively manage its risks it has to know its potential for risk. Many companies look to external consultants for the answer. Consultants have the obvious advantage of being able to look in from the outside with a more objective view. They also bring vast amounts of experience which has been gained by learning from others' past mistakes. This experience can help to guide an organization to success.

Common Software Risks

The first step in software risk management is to realize what the software risks are and what the potential for risk is. This information can be collected through the execution of a software risk analysis process. The analysis can be executed in either a survey or interview format. Typically it consists of key questions that reveal the likelihood for certain types of risk factors to occur. A simple risk analysis survey may collect risk potential information on the following details of the five common software risk categories.

1. Resource Effectiveness
   Skills: What is the likelihood that all the skills required to do the job will be present among the members of the project team?
   Project Management: Do project managers have the necessary levels of experience?

Staff: Are all members of the project team dedicated to a project or do they serve multiple project efforts?

2. Process Utilization

   Time to Market Delays: What is the chance that the product will be late?

   Standard Techniques and Methods: How effective is the execution of existing standards?

   Cost Estimates: Are budgets constantly being revisited due to improper cost estimating?

3. Applied Technology

   Evolving Technology: Are new technologies being introduced?

   Resources: Are there enough resources to adequately staff the projects?

   Development Automation Adequacy: Are the software engineers provided with the necessary tools to effectively do their jobs?

4. Deliverable Definition

   Functionality: Is the usefulness of the implemented functionality short lived?

   Impact of Quality and Reliability: What is the likelihood that the product will have significant problems?

   Business Reputation: Does the product contain the right functionality to support the business?

5. External Factors

   IS/User Management Conflicts: Is there likely to be disagreement regarding the deliverables?

   Definition of User Requirements: Are the requirements usually clearly stated?

   Business Commitments: Does the nature of the business suggest that frequent changes to specifications will occur?

Using this simple set of criteria, interviews and surveys should be conducted among various software management groups, including senior and mid-level management. Surveying different levels in the organization allows for a more comprehensive sampling. If the results contain significant variances, insights into the organization's perceptions and expectations will be revealed.

Within a very short timeframe an organization can highlight major areas of potential software risk. Using these data points, a risk profile can be established. The risk profile will show a summation of the collected risk data and will identify a company's top risk factors. Once risks have been identified it is possible to focus on improvement opportunities that will correct or minimize the risk factors. The improvement opportunities must then be prioritized. Prioritization is based upon the strategic success factors that are critical to the organization from a business perspective.

If strategic success factors are not defined from the analysis survey, then another set of data points is developed. The following strategic issues are a suggested set of factors which may be assessed from a business perspective:

- Improved delivery times to market
- Lowered software development costs

- ⮑ Lowered maintenance and production costs
- ⮑ Reduced technical staff
- ⮑ Minimized application backlog
- ⮑ Accurately estimated costs and schedules
- ⮑ Improved skill levels
- ⮑ Increased customer satisfaction
- ⮑ Increased use of commercial software
- ⮑ Efficient use of consultants and contractors
- ⮑ Optimized end-user software development
- ⮑ Optimized use of new technologies
- ⮑ All applications outsourced
- ⮑ Legacy applications outsourced

Once again the process can involve conducting interviews and surveys with senior and mid-level management. Each factor is evaluated on a scale of one to five, in order of priority. From the collected data a summary of critical strategies can be clearly defined.

After conducting both surveys we have two critical pieces of information: potential risk factors and critical business strategies. By matching potential risks with the business strategies, an organization can prioritize risks that need to be addressed. For example, the risk analysis may reveal that there are high risks involving significant time to market delays, inadequately defined requirements, and evolving technologies. The strategic goals survey may have revealed strategies necessary to improve delivery time, reduce cost, and stabilize production software. The analysis may suggest that more focus needs to be given to software stabilization before incurring additional risks associated with incorporating new technologies. The final step includes mapping the data to understand how these specific risks are serving as barriers to achieving the strategic goals.

All businesses face critical risk issues. In order to be successful a rigorous and well-thought path to managing these issues must be continuously developed. At the heart of it all is the notion of having key business measures. Industry gurus have told us for years that we need to measure what we manage. This has never been more true than in today's maturing software industry.

RETURN ON INVESTMENT

Another component of the successful business model includes the use of measures to monitor the dollars invested toward continued growth of the company. To stay in line with our notion of software as a unique business function, it seems only appropriate that we examine what data and what methods are available to us in order to measure our return on the technology investment.

Our discussion of return on investment (ROI) is an informal one. Our focus is not to enlighten the chief financial officer (CFO) of an organization but rather to develop a mindset on behalf of the manager in charge of the software business. Certainly a big part of what we want to identify is where we invest IS dollars. A standard list of categories includes investments made in resources (for example, training, hiring skilled labor), investments made in technologies, and investments made in improved processes. Two other fiscal practices to consider are chargeback and evaluation of software as an asset.

Many of the issues surrounding the value of the software deliverable may someday be addressed when a definitive and accurate formula is invented which will effectively measure return on investment for each technology dollar spent. However, the ability to consistently and accurately quantify return on investment for software technologies does not exist at the present time. Studies have been conducted by various vendors to demonstrate increases in productivity as a result of specific tool and/or method utilization. Quantifiable analysis has been done that shows positive increases in productivity as a result of rigorous execution of methods and tools. However, these studies lack the depth and breadth necessary to complete a standard ROI equation. These studies are narrow in their focus since they typically deal with direct costs only. Furthermore, the studies were conducted in a controlled environment where conditions were tightly controlled, and a number of other influencing factors were all aligned in a positive fashion. To compute a more realistic ROI we may consider the evaluation of the elements listed in Table 1.1.

This model obviously implies a time line since ongoing maintenance and ongoing system operations include the cost of those components over time. Additionally, components on the return side may not be fully realized in year one, but will have a positive result over time. A five year timeframe would be typical. For organizations seeking to justify or at least measure their technology investment, this formula may prove to be satisfactory. However, to quantify short-term, narrowly focused impacts on certain behaviors of tools, processes, and skill levels, an organization should realize that there may be an inconsistency in performance. Many other variables will come into play that either cannot be identified or cannot be controlled over a broader range of projects.

TABLE 1.1   Possible Software Investments Expected to Achieve a Return

Investment	Return
Technology purchases	Profits from enhanced revenue
Software development	Reduced operating costs
Ongoing maintenance	Reduced capital investments
Ongoing systems operations	Reduced inventory
Nonsystem operational charges	Indirect cost avoidance

Chargeback

Chargeback of IS expenditures to the various business operations within an organization has been used successfully since the middle of the 1970s. It is a common method used to manage the internal IS resource. Most organizations use chargeback as a way to accurately spread costs to fully recover internally the IS dollars spent across a number of business units that are utilizing the IS service.

Let's examine a simple model of chargeback. Company XYZ spends 12 million dollars a year on hardware, software, and technical services. There are four major business units that utilize these systems and technical services. Cost allocations are calculated based upon hardware useage. Software resources are charged on a full-time equivalent (FTE) basis. The result, if successfully computed, is an allocation of expense for the IS dollar across major business units.

Typically, the IS expenditure becomes a line item expense for each of the participating business units. This creates two dynamics that are inappropriate for what we want to achieve. First it suggests that the business units can or should somehow manage that expense. Secondly, it precludes the IS environment from functioning as a profit center. It disallows the notion of IS as a unique business operation.

Software as an Asset

By using the example of the XYZ company, we will modify how we allocate costs by putting a different spin on the chargeback schema. Instead of charging for total resource utilization, we will charge for business value. We will continue to chargeback for hardware utilization, but the software and the supporting services will be charged based on business functionality delivered to the user.

Assume that we have been able to successfully calculate the number of software "units" produced and delivered to the user. The calculation reveals that in the past we have been able to deliver 10,000 software "units" of business function to our customer. That delivery has involved 100 systems people and support personnel for a cost of 10 million dollars annually. Therefore each unit of business function delivered cost us $1000.

We further assume that the delivery of these units of software has satisfactorily met the quality standards put forth by the customer. We now enter into an agreement with our user stipulating that we will sell "units" of software for $1000 each. All things being equal, this formula will allow us to recover our costs. In this situation we are now in a more positive managing dynamic. The customer is not in a position to manage our expense since we are focusing the customer on a deliverable, not a line item expense. Secondly, we are now motivated to produce those software units in a more cost effective fashion. We may even turn a profit.

Furthermore, the customer knows what the costs are going to be for each software "unit" requested. The customer can build the appropriate business case and determine the ROI for that software. The IS organization can measure its own performance internally and determine its profitability and its return on investment.

Obviously the key measure becomes the software "unit". We need to be able to "unitize" the software deliverable. This is where Function Points provide us with one of its many virtues. Function Points may be used as a measure of functional value being delivered to the customer. A software "unit" can be translated to represent functional value being delivered. Functional value being delivered can be expressed in terms of Function Points.

In the example above, we talked about delivering 10,000 software units at a cost of $1000 per unit. We can express those 10,000 software units in terms of Function Points delivered and can equate the value to a cost per Function Point. Ultimately this would lead to a formula whereby an organization could successfully compute its software value and more accurately claim it as an asset.

STRATEGIC BUSINESS ALIGNMENT

We have talked about doing things right, understanding our strategic goals, and the software risk barriers to achieving those goals. We have discussed the need to reduce costs and improve time to market, but what about meeting the needs of the customer? How can functional metrics help?

It is important to do things right. It is equally important to do the right things. We can be the best developers that money and technology allow, but if we are not meeting market demand, there is little hope for our survival as a business. We must be strategically aligned with the business objectives.

There are several ways to monitor or to measure whether the right things are being done, but first we should identify what we mean by the right things. Right things refer to providing the business with the right information, at the right time, and with a high degree of accuracy. As we mentioned earlier, information is a company's true competitive advantage. An organization can hire the best and the brightest staff. We see industry talent moving from one company to the next every time we pick up a trade journal. Companies can also acquire the latest and greatest in technology. Faster machines and more sophisticated communication equipment are equally available to all. But, what about a company's data? That is the one resource that is uniquely its own. It is the one resource that it has complete control over. Therefore, it is the one resource that truly holds the key to improved business performance. Doing the right things equates to doing those things that will influence your business in a positive way and can be effectively managed or controlled.

How do we measure or assess our ability to do the right things? We know that there are a number of business performance indicators that tell us whether or not we are doing the right things. Measures such as profit levels and sales ratios are used to monitor a business on a daily, weekly, or monthly basis. Market share can also be a measure of success.

Another effective and economical way to measure whether or not we are delivering the right product is to ask our customers. Customer satisfaction surveys provide us with a better understanding of how effectively and efficiently we are meeting customer demand. Are we putting the right functionality into our customers' hands at the right time and in an easily useable format?

The challenge for software developers is to understand how to measure whether or not they are doing the right things during the software development process. Fortunately, these measurement opportunities occur at natural intervals during the phases of the development lifecycle. We have the opportunity to measure during requirements, design, build, and testing.

First and foremost, we need to assume that customers know what they want and have a clear understanding of the product that they want delivered and the information requirements necessary to run their business. Software professionals cannot be expected to build quality software from poorly defined requirements. The job of the software professional is to deliver the defined, required data, in an agreeable format, and within specified time and location parameters. This must be done in as technically feasible a way as current resources will allow. It is the responsibility of the customer to be clear and articulate about needs and desires. The customer must bear the risk for developing inaccurate requirements. That is not to say that the customer is responsible for all the sins of poor definition and requirements. It is simply to say that the software developers are geared toward running the software development business; they are not in the business of running the company

Certainly, there are occasions when it is critical to have the technical staff involved in defining requirements. Software professionals can and should inform and educate business people about data processing capabilities and possibilities, and assist with alternative requirement decisions considering preliminary cost trade-offs. If skilled personnel are available within IS to participate in defining the business solutions because they possess either the knowledge or the means to gain that knowledge, then, by all means, they should participate. The more clearly the requirements are stated, the more productive the development team will be in delivering those requirements.

So how can Function Points support this need? As we learned earlier, Function Points provide us with a vehicle to measure the functionality being delivered to the end-user. They provide a sizing mechanism that allows us to measure that functionality in specific and consistent terms. The value of functionality is determined by the market, but the defining and the sizing of that functionality can be done using Function Point techniques.

CHAPTER

2

MEASURING
PERFORMANCE

INTRODUCTION

In Chapter 1 we discussed the need to consider the software business unit as distinct and unique within an organization. Based on the simple shift in our thinking about how we manage the software environment, we identified the need to manage that environment using software measures. After all, we know that successful businesses measure successfully. The inspiring story of the Ford Motor Company (*The Whiz Kids*, J. Byrne, Doubleday, 1992) and its ability to turn itself around after World War II, to compete with the likes of General Motors, was directly attributable to its instituting a rigorous set of measures by which it could monitor its business practices and make informed decisions regarding key business strategies.

Having accepted the fact that we need to manage software using measurement, we now move on to the principles of software measurement. What do we measure and how do we apply those measures?

It is not our intent to present a complete discourse on the fundamentals of establishing and managing a successful measurement program; however, it is important to present specific measurement concepts as a way to position Function Points, and to demonstrate the significance of Function Points in the measuring of software.

This chapter presents a basic software process assessment model that can be used in the discussion of commonly practiced assessment methodologies. We will review the availability of industry data and the cautions that need to be exercised when examining that data. Different types of measures will be presented including business and technical measures. Finally, we will discuss other functional measurement methods being used in the field today. All of these methods and techniques are discussed in the context of how Function Points support or interact with them.

ASSESSING SOFTWARE PROCESS PERFORMANCE LEVELS

We are in the "business" of developing software. It is either our primary business or it is a function that we support within a business community. If we are to be successful in the development of software, we need to focus on our capacity to produce that software. This requires us to have the ability to adequately assess our software process performance levels.

Chapter 1 discussed the need to understand our software risk potential. Now, with much greater rigor, we need to understand the specific risks, know where and when they occur in the software process, and know if we are improving the process as we implement new techniques, methods, and tools.

To understand how we are going to assess our risk potential or our ability to deliver software, we present a very simple and yet effective model for software process assessment (Figure 2.1).

Our focus is on assessing our current software practices. The assessment model depicted in Figure 2.1 suggests that software practices are to be evaluated based on qualitative data. That data allows us to understand our current process capabilities. Using this data we can identify current proficiencies and inadequacies and ultimately identify opportunities for software improvements. As improvements are identified we can update our current practices while continuing to make assessments.

ASSESSMENT METHODOLOGIES

There are a number of assessment methodologies available in the commercial marketplace. While their differences can be significant, and may cause one to hesitate

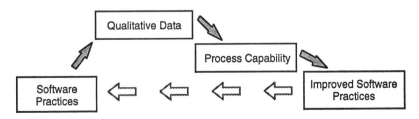

FIGURE 2.1   Qualitative Process Assessment Flow

in the decision to assess, as a general rule it is better to assess, regardless of the method, than not to assess at all.

The most popular assessment technique is the Software Engineering Institute (SEI) assessment methodology developed by Watts Humphrey. Used mostly by the Department of Defense (DoD) and DoD contractors, it uses a model for software measurement maturity, called the Capability Maturity Model (CMM). This model is represented by five descriptive levels. Associated with each level are Key Process Areas. In order to progress up the maturity scale you must meet all the criteria of the preceding level. The five levels and the associated Key Process Areas are noted in Table 2.1.

Note that there are no Key Process Areas associated with Level 1. Level 1 is where you will be if you fail to meet all the criteria associated with Level 2. It is in-

TABLE 2.1   SEI Capability Maturity Model Key Process Areas

Level	Description Key Process Areas
5	Optimizing
	Process Change Management
	Technology Innovation
	Defect Prevention
4	Managed
	Quality Management
	Process Measurement
3	Defined
	Peer Reviews
	Intergroup Coordination
	Software Product Engineering
	Integrated Software Management
	Training Program
	Organization Process Definition
	Organization Process Focus
2	Repeatable
	Software Configuration Management
	Software Quality Assurance
	Software Subcontract Management
	Software Project Tracking
	Software Project Planning
	Requirements Management
1	Initial

teresting to note that the majority of companies assessed to date have fallen into the Level 1 and Level 2 categories.

Equating this to our assessment model we see that the SEI is heavily focused on the qualitative aspect of process assessment as well. There are no quantitative measures directly associated with the SEI maturity model. In other words, there is no opportunity, based on the results of the assessment, to determine the quantitative value of moving from a Level 1 organization to a Level 2 organization. These measures would have to be gathered in parallel to the SEI process in order to quantify possible improvements realized by progressing up the SEI scale.

This SEI model is a static process assessment model. The assessment process and resulting recommendations for improving that process require an organization to begin at the lowest level. It must satisfy all the requirements at that level before realizing opportunities in the next stage of maturity. The benefit of this process is the delivery of a prioritized path to process improvement. The fundamental flaw in this approach is that the process fails to acknowledge isolated "above the norm" performance levels that may have been achieved. Achievements at the higher levels are not highlighted and, therefore, result in possible opportunity lost situations.

We can compare the static SEI model with a dynamic model for process improvement. A dynamic model should allow an organization to examine its current performance, to identify areas of inadequacy and areas of proficiency, and to then focus on improvement. The added component in the dynamic model is the presence of quantitative data.

To examine this in greater detail, we have expanded our process assessment model as you can see in Figure 2.2. This more dynamic model examines the software practices using two distinct measures; one involving the assessment of quantitative data and the other involving the assessment of qualitative data. Quantitative data realizes factors such as the size of the software, the effort required to deliver or

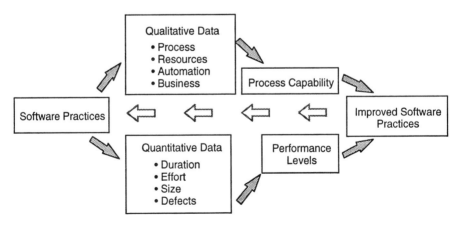

FIGURE 2.2   A Complete Process Assessment Model

support that software, the overall duration or time required to produce the software, and the number of defects, usually pre- and post-implementation.

From this data we calculate performance levels. Common expressions of performance levels include productivity and quality ratings. If we are measuring the size of our software in Function Points, then we would express a productivity result as the number of Function Points produced per person/month. This measure of productivity becomes one of several measures that allows us to compare our performance to industry standards, as we will see later in this chapter.

If we choose to measure a variety of our software systems or software project efforts, we will soon establish what is commonly referred to as a baseline. This baseline provides us with a variety of performance level data points based on varying degrees of productivity and quality performance. Not all efforts within an organization will demonstrate the same rate of performance. As shown in Figure 2.3, the result of plotting a variety of projects results in a display of various productivity levels, or delivery rates.

It is important that we recognize and acknowledge the varying degrees of process performance and ultimately understand the causes for the variations in performance. This is where the qualitative data becomes critical. The qualitative data describes how we build and maintain our systems.

Referencing our model once again, we see that the qualitative data is expressed in terms of the software process we use, the resource capacity we own, the level of automation in our development environment, and the nature of the business environment. These are often referred to as influences. In actuality there are any number of influences that ultimately impact the productivity and quality levels of our software development performance.

In terms of effectively capturing and analyzing qualitative data, the SEI per-

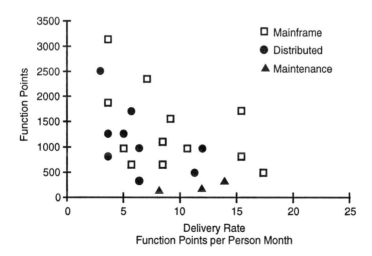

FIGURE 2.3 Representative project data points plotted on a productivity graph

forms very well. Where the SEI process falls short is that it provides no quantitative measurement of the resulting assessment. We assume that if we move up the SEI maturity scale, we will increase our levels of productivity and quality: but without quantitative measures, we really never know for certain.

The dynamic software assessment model, which includes a quantitative component, allows us to maximize our efforts by concentrating our resources on those elements of the process that work well for us and focus our attention on those elements of the process that are quantified as weaknesses. We do not become pigeonholed into a particular predefined maturity level. We begin the process by seeking our own level of strength or weakness and then plot our improvement strategies.

To bring this discussion back to the topic of Function Points, the crucial lesson learned here is that Function Points are just one of a number of required measures. There is little doubt in any practitioner's mind that Function Points are the key metric here; however, Function Points, in and of themselves, do not reveal much without the use and the combination of other metrics.

BASELINING AN ORGANIZATION

Baselining is a common practice in organizations that are conducting software measurement practices. It involves the collection and analysis of data across numerous projects and/or systems. The purpose is to collect enough data so that a statistically sound reference point can be derived. This baseline data is then used in a variety of ways to monitor ongoing progress. Baseline data is collected either by a concentrated effort which extends over a relatively short timeframe (one to three months) or over a longer timeframe, typically on an annualized basis.

Two common baseline types include a systems or application baseline and a delivery baseline. The systems baseline is simply a collection of system size data and other measures such as number of support resources and number of support requirements or requests. The data captured with a system baseline is commonly used in the planning of support resources that may be required in the coming months and years. Additionally, this data can be used to assess the value of reengineering certain systems that are either costly to support or that tend to have major shifts in functionality.

The delivery baseline is typically comprised of recently completed software development and enhancement projects. Software size and effort to produce are plotted, and resulting delivery rates are computed. Often this data is segmented by delivery type, technology used, development platform, and/or application type.

Figure 2.4 shows selected baseline projects for client server (distributed) projects within an organization. Graphical representations such as this can be very informative and can prompt a desire to gather more information. One quick glance at the chart in Figure 2.4 piques our curiosity, and we want to know why we have the variations in delivery rate across similarly sized projects. In addition, we want to know where we stand relative to the rest of the industry.

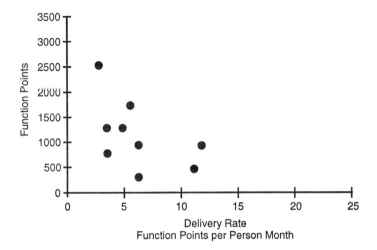

FIGURE 2.4   Selected client server projects plotted on a productivity graph

INDUSTRY COMPARISONS

Industry data representing productivity and software quality performance is of interest to everyone these days. Companies desire industry data for many different reasons. They want to understand how they compare to like businesses. They want to be capable of showing improvement relative to industry trends. They need to know "industry best practices" and how they will realize when they have arrived at that point.

The desire for industry data is so great that many companies are willing to accept publicly available industry data at face value. Many providers and publishers of industry data have collected information that has not been validated, is not current, or is incomplete. Depending on how a company uses this information, potentially disastrous results can occur if decisions are made based on data that is not truly representative of industry trends. To avoid such pitfalls, the following criteria should be applied when obtaining industry data:

1. *For what industry is the data representative, and what is the mix of data?* Typically industry data is a result of numerous data points that have been collected across a wide variety of industries. There is often no balance in the data; one or two industries represent the majority of data points. If they happen to coincide with your industry then you are fortunate; otherwise, they may be of little or no significance.

2. *What is the time period represented by the data?* Vendors claiming to have thousands of projects in their data base are not as quick to tell you that the data has been collected over an extended period of time. If you are looking for current data, you should realize that the sampling of current data will be relatively small and may not be representative of thousands of projects.

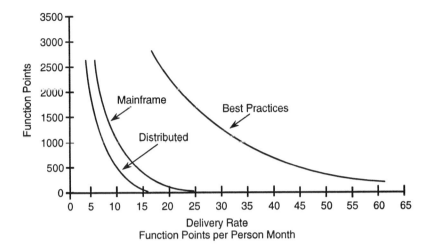

FIGURE 2.5   Comparative Industry Baselines

3. *How valid is the data?* Often, data is collected from many sources. This limits the likelihood that the data has been validated. In addition, much of the data is of an empirical nature and, therefore, has some level of distortion.

Displays of industry data (Figure 2.5) are typically representative of data collected from a range of projects within a given timeframe. Different data points are usually presented to represent different technologies or environments. On the chart in Figure 2.5 we see data points for distributed projects, mainframe projects, and best practices. Frequently best practices data is a based on modeled data, not collected data.

The true value of having this data available may be best demonstrated in Figure 2.6. Here we have combined the industry data for distributed projects and imposed that industry benchmark on the graph from Figure 2.4 which depicted selected client server (distributed) projects. This gives an organization an immediate view of where it is relative to the industry. Of course, the organization needs to conduct a rigorous assessment process to understand the variations it is experiencing. Having completed that assessment, they can then move toward the path of improved software processing. The organization can continue to use this type of graphical representation to understand its improvement trends.

MEASUREMENT OPPORTUNITIES

Obtaining Function Point counts provides the basis for creating a variety of valuable software process performance and quality measures. Function Point values can stand alone as high level monitors of the application domain, or they can be com-

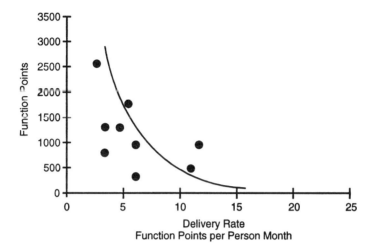

FIGURE 2.6 Selected client server projects compared with a distributed project industry baseline curve

bined with other measures to provide a robust opportunity to effectively manage the software environment. They are also considered to be the normalizing measure that allows for comparisons among industry segments.

In order to be successful, software measurement must focus on the needs of the organization, it must be supported throughout the organization, and it must be a value added tool by which to manage the software process. It is fairly common to hear software measurement specialists talk about the high failure rate of measurement programs. Typically those failures can be traced back to the shortcomings in one or more of the aforementioned success criteria.

Function Points—As a Stand-alone Metric

As organizations become increasingly cost conscious they are concerned with gaining control of their entire applications domain. The need then arises to measure their portfolios of applications. Often this is expressed in terms of needing to understand the value of their software assets. If they are aware of the benefits of functional metrics, then their choice will be to establish a portfolio baseline count using Function Points. Of course to count an entire portfolio of applications using the Function Point method would be cost prohibitive in many medium and large size organizations, thus alternative approaches are sought. Often, partial application portfolios are developed using Function Point counts, and the remaining applications are sized using approximation techniques.

Portfolio counts provide an organization with size data for comparing applications and potentially making comparisons to purchased software packages. They are also useful as a base measure to determine resource allocations for long-term planning. Typically, this information is gathered over a period of time and is usually part of the application baselining efforts.

Having established a baseline count of applications, it is very common to support that count by continuing the counting process on subsequent projects that will influence the established Function Point count for a particular system. This is a way to determine the growth of the application over time and is valuable information when planning for support resources or when considering reengineering of certain applications.

Function Points and Core Metrics

There exists in the software measurement practice a commonly accepted set of core metrics. The core measures include Function Points plus four other metrics: level of effort, costs, defects, and duration.

Level of effort includes all time recorded in support of the software delivery effort. For a new development or enhancement project, level of effort includes all time officially recorded to that project, including project management time and any unpaid overtime. For maintenance projects, level of effort includes all time associated with supporting the system. Currently there are no industry standards for collecting and calculating *costs*. The commonly used cost factors include labor, training, contract labor, travel expenses, management, and overhead. Two categories of *defects* are commonly utilized, pre-implementation defects, and post-implementation defects. *Duration* refers to the overall elapsed scheduled time for developing or enhancing an application or for supporting a system.

Similar to the three primary colors, this core set of metrics spawns a spectrum of commonly accepted industry measures. Common calculations are listed in Table 2.2.

Function Points and Industry Data

Increasingly Function Points are gaining in popularity, based on the availability of industry data. Much industry data is based on Function Point measures. The value of using Function Points is in the consistency of the metric. If we use lines of code to compare ourselves to other organizations we face the problems associated with the inconsistencies in counting lines of code. Differences in language complexity

TABLE 2.2   Common Industry Software Measure

Type	Metrics	Measure
Productivity	Function Points / Effort	Function Points per person month
Responsiveness	Function Points / Duration	Function Points per calendar month
Quality	Defect / Function Points	Defects per Function Points
Business	Costs / Function Points	Cost per Function Point

levels and inconsistency in counting rules quickly lead us to conclude that line of code counting, even within an organization, can be problematic and ineffective. This is not the case with Function Points.

Function Points also serve many different measurement types. Again, lines of code measure the value of the rate of delivery during the coding phase. Function Points measure the value of the entire deliverable from a productivity perspective, a quality perspective, and a cost perspective.

Figure 2.7A, B, C, D depicts several industry graphical displays of different delivery rates.

FUNCTIONAL METRIC METHODOLOGIES

Function Points

The Function Point methodology has not gone unchallenged over the past ten years. Due to various criticisms regarding the methodology's possible shortcomings, there have been several attempts to invent a better mousetrap. The criticisms tend to originate from people in the scientific, telecommunications, and real-time/embedded software communities. Their collective concern centers around the fact that Function Points were developed in and for an IS world and do not consider all the elements of complexity that are inherent in other types of software.

It is true that Function Points were developed in an information systems environment and, therefore, the rules and guidelines do support a flavor of software development that is oriented toward that environment. Practitioners generally agree that the guidelines are presented in the language of the IS developer, but they are flexible enough to be adaptable to other software environments. Perhaps this is best demonstrated by the recent changes in the IFPUG *Counting Practices Guidelines* that were made to align themselves with common graphical user interface (GUI) terms and technologies. The method was not changed in this instance, but the narrative describing how to use this method in a GUI environment was successfully modified.

The Function Point methodology originated in the mid1970s at IBM. It was born out of the need to establish a more effective and predictable measure of system size, which could be used to better predict or estimate delivery of software. In 1979, Allan Albrecht first introduced the methodology at a joint Share/Guide conference. From 1979 to 1984 continued statistical analysis was performed on the method, and refinements were made. The result is the Function Point methodology we use today.

The methodology involves the identification of transactional and data function types that process or store groups of logically related data or control information. Once identified, the function types are weighted based on several elements including the amount of data and the complexity of the data relationships. An unadjusted count is derived from the sum of the data types and their assigned weights and then adjusted using a set of fourteen General Systems Characteristics.

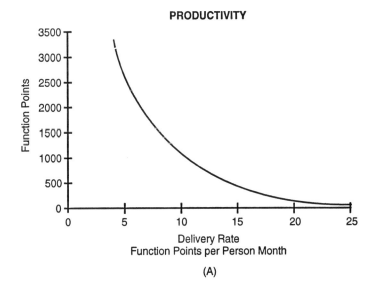

(A)

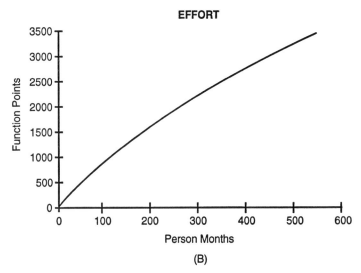

(B)

FIGURE 2.7   Industry Baseline Curves

The General Systems Characteristics are intended to value additional functionality of the system that includes such things as user friendliness, transaction rates, performance, and reuseability. A final Function Point count is then computed using the unadjusted count and the total value of the summed General Systems Characteristics.

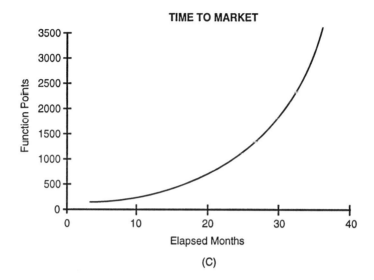

(C)

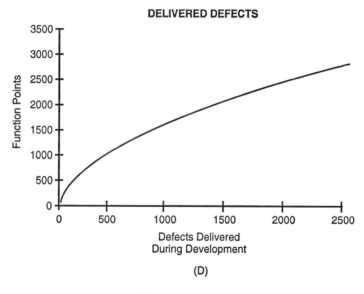

(D)

FIGURE 2.7 *Continued*

To date there have been no functional measurement methods introduced that suggest that Function Point methods, as we know them, should not continue to receive widespread usage across various software development environments. There has been no form of functional measurement presented that parallels the proven statistical accuracy of Function Point analysis or that has gained the same widespread acceptance that Function Points have received. However, there are several other functional measurement techniques that have demonstrated potential value and certainly deserve mention.

Mark II Method

Charles Symons is credited with the development of the British Mark II Method of Functional Measurement. In 1988 he published a description of his method and in it stated his concerns regarding shortcomings in the Function Point methodology and suggested the following reforms regarding the current version of Function Points:

⇨ Reduce the subjectivity in dealing with files by measuring the number of entities and their performance as they move through the data structure

⇨ Modify the Function Point method to compute the same numeric totals regardless of application boundary as a single system or as a set of related subsystems

⇨ Focus on the effort required to produce the functionality rather than on the value of the functionality delivered to the users

⇨ Add six additional complexity factors to the fourteen General System Characteristics.

As recently as the fall of 1994, Paul Goodwin, Technical Director for TOK Brameur in the UK, presented his recent experience using Mark II and made some interesting comparisons to Function Points. He concluded that

> . . . both methods use the same basic parameters in their calculations. Mark II makes use of fewer parameters and is thought to be conceptually simpler to use. Performance, based on effort and size correlation, was about equal using the two methods, but greater variations are experienced on small projects when using the Mark II method.

The use of the Mark II method has been almost exclusively centered in the UK. The lack of wide-scale usage has limited the acceptance of the method due to limited availability of statistically sound conclusions. The presentation by Paul Goodwin does demonstrate, however, that in some environments the method is successfully being used.

Feature Points

Capers Jones developed an experimental method for applying Function Point methods to system software including operating systems and telecom systems. The method, known as Feature Points, was developed in direct response to the scientific community's skepticism that Function Points would accurately measure the real-time software work product. Since first being introduced in 1986, this method has been experimentally applied in a number of scientific communities. Several organizations have applied this process very successfully, including Perkin Elmer, Instrumentation Labs, and Motorola.

The Feature Point method is a superset of the Function Point method. It makes use of an additional component, algorithms, adding to the set of the five Function Point components: inputs, outputs, inquiries, external interface files, and internal logical files. In concert with the other Function Point components, the algorithm component is assigned a weighted value. When using the Feature Point method, the IFPUG values assigned to internal files are reduced.

Admittedly this technique is still considered experimental. There is not enough statistical evidence to conclude that it can be applied in a consistent fashion. In those instances where the method was successfully applied and used as a software sizing mechanism, the practitioners demonstrated consistency within their own environments.

The potential shortcoming of this method is centered around the definition of algorithms. Capers Jones has developed a list of supplemental rules for determining what an algorithm is, but his best attempts still have not gone past generalized definitions. This puts the onus on the practitioner to define algorithms that will be applicable to the working environment. Once a consistent definition is achieved, the remainder of the process tends to work very effectively.

The perceived value of this method is that it has aligned itself with the well-defined Function Point methodology Therefore, the practitioner of Feature Points does not have to learn two sets of rules. Its close alignment with the Function Point method suggests the future possibility of deriving correlation between the two methods, allowing for comparisons to industry benchmark data. IS application Function Points and Feature Points tend to be similar and the additional algorithm component provides a dimension that measures the internal complexity inherent in some scientific or real-time applications.

3D Function Points

3D Function Points were initiated in 1989 and publicly introduced by the Boeing Computer Services Software Metrics Team in 1991. Similar to the origins of Feature Points, they were in part born out of the perception that the Function Point method was not a metric that could serve the scientific and real-time community very well. Secondly, 3D was developed in response to the call for a technology-independent size metric suitable for all domains.

The 3D method is based on the premise that the application problem can be expressed in three dimensions: data, function, and control. Each dimension contains some of the characteristics that create complexity in a problem. Sometimes one dimension dominates, but all dimensions of the problem must be analyzed if accurate measurement is desired.

The 3D method identifies characteristics from each dimension that can be measured directly. Data strong problems are typically associated with IS/business software environments. The data dimension characteristics are taken directly from the IFPUG guidelines and include evaluation of inputs, outputs, inquiries, internal logical files and external interface files. Function strong problems are associated with scientific/engineering environments. The characteristics of the functional dimension include the number and the complexity of functions that represent internal processing required to transform input data into output data and the sets of semantic statements that govern the process. Control strong problems are associated with real-time environments. The characteristics of the control dimension includes system states and transitions.

The steps in the 3D process include the identification of measurable characteristics from each dimension that contribute to the overall problem complexity. Rules are applied to the counting and assigning of complexity levels for the identified characteristics and a final summation is computed. The intent of the Boeing presentation was to introduce the method and gain support among the functional measurement community. As with any experimental metric, continued attempts to validate this method are necessary.

3

FUNCTION POINT ANALYSIS

INTRODUCTION

The Function Point counting rules have been reviewed, clarified, and made significantly more consistent since they were initially introduced by Allan Albrecht of IBM in 1979. The International Function Point Users Group (IFPUG) promulgates the *Counting Practices Manual*, which contains the current standards and guidelines for the counting process. This chapter will discuss the IFPUG process for counting Function Points, the types of counts, and the boundaries or the software process being measured. The subsequent chapters will describe the data function types, the transaction function types, the general system characteristics, and the calculations involved.

THE FUNCTION POINT PROCESS

Function Point analysis is an accepted standard for the measurement of software size. Function Point analysis is a normalizing factor for software comparison, much the same as other standard units of size; for example, cubic yards or cubic meters, gallons or liters, pounds or kilograms. Function Points on their own suggest nothing about value or cost. Other factors must also be considered when estimating cost, value, or resource requirements for software development, acquisition, or maintenance. This does not diminish the value of Function Point analysis but places it in perspective with other consistent standards of measurement: a yard of beach-front property is usually worth significantly more than a frontage yard of inaccessible land; a gallon of gasoline is currently valued higher than a gallon of water; a pound of steak costs more than a pound of potatoes.

Function Point analysis can be applied throughout the software development and maintenance process to quantify application functionality provided to the users of that software. The measurement is independent of the methodology and technology applied to the development and/or maintenance. The total process used to size Function Points can be summarized by the following seven steps:

1. Determine the type of Function Point count*
2. Identify the application boundary*
3. Identify all data functions and their complexity
4. Identify all transactional functions and their complexity
5. Determine the Unadjusted Function Point count
6. Determine the Value Adjustment Factor—fourteen General System Characteristics
7. Calculate the final Adjusted Function Point Count

This is a lot to assimilate without any additional information. Let's begin our discussion with an example of a purchased application which does nothing more than maintain the phone numbers of individuals at a location. We will also limit ourselves to the first four steps above and exclude any complexity assessment for the data and transactional functions. We are conducting an application Function Point count and determining the application size. The application boundary separates the application being measured from the user domain and/or other independent applications. The data functions relate to the logical data stored and available for update and retrieval. The transactional functions perform the processes of updates, retrieval, outputs, etc. (transactions you would expect to see in a process model). Figure 3.1 illustrates a sample of the functional components included in the sample application.

As previously discussed, step one was to determine the type of Function Point count. There are three types of Function Point counts:

Development Project Function Point counts

Enhancement Project Function Point counts

Application Function Point counts

*Discussed in this chapter

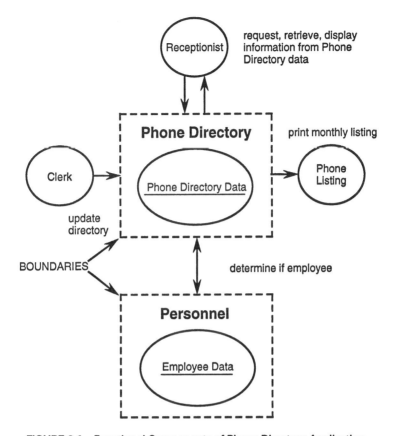

FIGURE 3.1   Functional Components of Phone Directory Application

We will discuss these later in the chapter. We counted an existing application with-out regard to its history of development. We do not know how long ago it was de-veloped or whether any previous enhancements or changes have occurred.

Step two was to identify the application boundary. Our boundary separates the Clerk, the Receptionist, the produced Phone Listing, and the Personnel applica-tion from the Phone Directory application.

Step three requires the identification of the data functions. The Phone Direc-tory Data, an internal logical file (ILF), is maintained within the boundary of the ap-plication. The Employee Data, an external interface file (EIF), is maintained within the boundary of the Personnel application and is used by the Phone Directory appli-cation solely for reference data.

Step four requires the identification of the transactional functions. The Clerk updates, as an external input (EI), Phone Directory Data. The Phone Listing is gen-erated as an external output (EO). The Receptionist requests the retrieval and dis-play, an external inquiry (EQ), of information currently stored in Phone Directory

Data internal logical file, although information could also be retrieved from an external interface file such as Employee data.

These, once again, are only examples of the functional components within an application. If you can understand these concepts, you are well on your way to counting Function Points. We will provide much more extensive definitions and many more examples later.

The size of an application in Function Points can be used together with consideration of project attributes (such as skill level of the developers, development languages to be used, the methodology and technology to be applied, and the tasks to be performed) in order to estimate cost and resource requirements. Consequently, Function Point analysis can be introduced early in the estimation process and reevaluated whenever there is a change of scope or as a new phase of the development process occurs. Since Function Points should represent the functionality that the user (end-user, marketing personnel, business analyst, buyer) requests, it is our view that it is never too early to perform a functional analysis. In fact, gathering the interested parties together early in the software project proposal phase to achieve a functional analysis will ultimately make the developers' job easier and will ensure that the users state their case for what it is that they want developed.

The process for counting Function Points will vary based upon the particular status of an application. Less information is typically available early in the development process; significantly more information is available as an application is developed and delivered. Early in the process, the only information available could be verbal. During the development process, the information available to assist in counting increases to include some of the following potential documents which are helpful in determining Function Point counts:

- ↜ Project proposals
- ↜ Requirement documents
- ↜ High-level system diagrams
- ↜ Entity relationship diagrams
- ↜ Functional specifications
- ↜ System specifications
- ↜ Logical data models
- ↜ Database layout
- ↜ Process models
- ↜ Program/module specifications
- ↜ Screens/screen prints for on-line systems
- ↜ File layouts
- ↜ Copies of reports or report layouts
- ↜ User manuals

↝ Training materials
↝ System HELP

Types of Counts

The first step, identified above, in the Function Point counting process is to determine the type of Function Point count to be conducted. Three types of counts exist:

1. *Development Project Function Point Counts* measure the functionality provided to end-users with the first installation of the application. Development Project Function Point Counts include the functionality which will be counted in the initial Application Function Point Count as well as any functionality required for data conversion. If we were replacing the Phone Directory application discussed in Figure 3.1 with a newly developed application, we would count the functionality provided by the new application. We should, as well, count the conversion functionality required by the users to convert data which resided in the old data files to the new data files. A Development Function Point Count must often be updated as the development process proceeds. These would not be "start from scratch" counts, but they would validate previously identified functionality and attempt to capture added functionality, commonly called "scope creep". Counts could occur during the phases shown in Figure 3.2

2. *Enhancement Project Function Point Counts* measure modifications to existing applications and include the combined functionality provided to users by adding new functions, deleting old functions, and changing existing functions. Conversion functionality could also exist in an enhancement project. After an enhancement, the Application Function Point Count must be revised to reflect the appropriate changes in the application's functionality.

3. *Application Function Point Counts* measure an installed application. They are also referred to as baseline or installed counts and provide counts of the current functionality provided to end-users by the application. The total of an

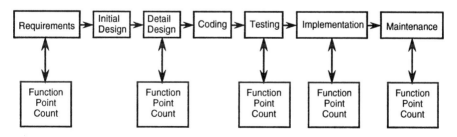

FIGURE 3.2   Function Point Counting During the Software Life Cycle

activity's Application Function Point Counts typically represents all installed applications that are currently being maintained.

Defining the Boundaries

Boundaries indicate the border between the project or application being measured and external applications or the user domain. IFPUG has defined specific rules that are used when identifying boundaries. The rules are as follows:

- ↪ The boundary is based on the user's point of view. The user should be able to define the scope of the application.
- ↪ The boundary between related applications is based on separate business functionality and not on technological implementation. Several examples are appropriate. Microsoft Office consists of Word, Excel, PowerPoint, and Access which are each separate applications within the Microsoft Office suite. A generic example, System Alpha, consists of an on-line data entry process, which is followed by a nightly batch file update process; System Alpha is a single application.
- ↪ The initial application boundary for an application being enhanced changes with the enhancement. Added functionality may expand the boundary, and deleted functionality may reduce the boundary. Changed functionality may change the function point size of the application. This rule is meant to indicate that an enhancement does not become its own application boundary.

Development Projects and Enhancement Projects often include more than a single application. In these cases, multiple application boundaries would be identified and separately counted. Function Point counting is often depicted by a version of the graphic displayed in Figure 3.3.

It is extremely important that all facets of Function Point counting be accomplished consistently. However, Function Point counting has little benefit if counting is accomplished consistently but incorrectly. This is particularly true when identifying application boundaries. Boundaries should not be established at the application software program or module level. Function Points should be counted at a higher application level. It is also possible to count at a level that is too high. For example, an accounting system might consist of several separate applications such as Accounts Receivable, General Ledger, and Accounts Payable (Figure 3.4). Likewise, a military weapon system usually consists of many subordinate but independent applications, which are separately developed, maintained, and utilized such as a Radar System, Command Decision System, and Missile System (Figure 3.5).

IFPUG has published additional definitions and hints to be utilized in identifying boundaries. We will address the types of counts and boundaries in the following chapters as well as in the case studies.

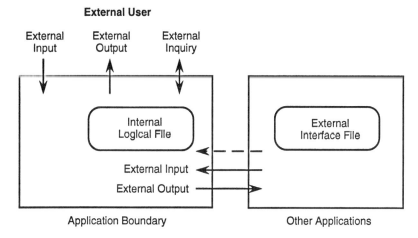

FIGURE 3.3   Function Point Counting Components

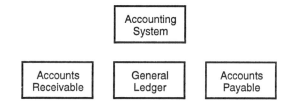

FIGURE 3.4   An Accounting System with Three Applications

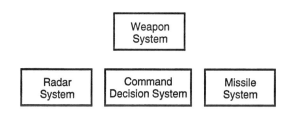

FIGURE 3.5   A Weapon System with Three Applications

CHAPTER

4

DATA FUNCTION TYPES

INTRODUCTION

When experienced Function Point counters size an application in Function Points, they experience the greatest degree of difficulty in identifying the data function types. Data functions relate to logical data stored and available for update and retrieval. Data types are identified as either internal logical files (ILFs) or external interface files (EIFs). They both are user identifiable groups of logically related data or control information. As such they are logical groupings and not physical representations of those groupings of data. It is possible, but unlikely, that the logical grouping will match the physical implementation. Consequently, ILFs and EIFs should be counted in an identical manner regardless of the database structure. An application should be counted with the same number of ILFs and EIFs whether the physical file structure is constructed with flat files, an IDMS database, an IMS database, a relational database, DB2 tables or objects; obviously, the delivery and maintenance requirements and rates may be different. ILFs are maintained within the boundary of the application being counted, and EIFs are read and/or referenced only within the boundary of the application being counted but maintained within a different application boundary. This chapter will describe the International Function

Point Users Group (IFPUG) definitions, rules, and guidelines for identifying both ILFs and EIFs. More detailed guidance is contained within the IFPUG *Counting Practices Manual.* The previous chapter discussed the IFPUG process for counting Function Points, the types of counts, and the boundaries or the software process being measured. The following chapters will describe the transaction function types, the general system characteristics, and the calculations involved.

DATA FUNCTION TYPES

The total process used to size Function Points was presented in the previous chapter and is repeated here. The counting process can be summarized by the following seven steps:

1. Determine the type of Function Point count
2. Identify the application boundary
3. Identify all data functions and their complexity*
4. Identify all transactional functions and their complexity
5. Determine the Unadjusted Function Point count
6. Determine the Value Adjustment Factor—fourteen General System Characteristics
7. Calculate the final Adjusted Function Point Count

Remember that the application boundary separates the application being measured from the user domain and/or other independent applications. The data functions relate to the logical data stored and available for update and retrieval. The transactional functions, external inputs (EIs), external outputs (EOs) and external inquiries (EQs), perform the processes of updates, retrieval, outputs, etc. (transactions you would expect to see in a process model). We attempt to count data functions first for two reasons:

1. First, we must know which ILFs and EIFs are maintained and/or referenced by each transactional function in order to assign each its own complexity rating. We will discuss the complexity ratings for all functions later, but each data and transactional function will be assigned a weight of low, average, or high based on standard matrices.
2. Second, by identifying the files first, we can validate their original designations as ILFs or EIFs as we proceed to identify the transactional functions.

Recall Figure 3.1 from the previous chapter and remember that the Phone Directory data, an internal logical file (ILF), was maintained within the boundary of

*Discussed in this chapter

the application. The Employee data, an external interface file (EIF), was maintained within the boundary of the Personnel application and was used by the Phone Directory application solely for reference data. Consequently, in order to be counted as an ILF, the logical grouping of data must be updated or maintained by at least one of the external inputs (EIs) within the application.

The ILF usually will be read or referenced by an EO or EQ or another EI, or that capability will be planned. That read or reference could occur within another application, but it is uncommon that a read or reference would not occur in the application being counted. To be counted as an EIF, some of the data from that logical grouping, though maintained elsewhere, must be read or referenced by at least one EI, EO, or EQ within the application being counted.

Internal Logical Files

An *internal logical file* (*ILF*) is a user identifiable group of logically related data or control information maintained through an elementary process of the application within the boundary of the application.

The terms used in this definition are described below:

- ↪ *User identifiable* refers to the specific requirements that an experienced user would define for the application; for example, a checking account record might be required in a banking application.

- ↪ *Logically related* refers to the requirement that each group should fit logically together within the descriptions provided. An ILF should not be dependent upon or attributive to another ILF in order to maintain its existence. Groups should be merged as necessary, particularly those that were created for performance or implementation reasons. ILFs are typically represented by entity types in second or third normal form. The data analysis equivalent to such high level logical groupings are a singular named data store on a data flow diagram. As an example, an address table would probably belong to a higher level such as a client file, a billing file, an inventory location file, or an employee file.

- ↪ *Data* refers to the collection of facts and/or figures maintained within the application; for example, check number, amount, date, payee, memo entry, and account might be maintained in the checking account record for each check written.

- ↪ *Control information* is data used by the application to influence an elementary process of the application being counted; in the case of ILFs, these data, rules, or parameters are stored and maintained within the application: for example, control data is maintained in print manager; edit data is maintained in order to reject improper or inappropriate input data; dates and times are maintained by the users to establish the timing of events; certain thresholds are established to control an event such as setting the temperature on a thermostat to control the timing of heating or air conditioning.

↩ *Maintained* refers to the fact that the data is created, modified, or deleted through an elementary process of the application. The data or control data could be maintained through such transactions as add, bill, change, delegate, evaluate, fail, grant, hold, populate, revise, update, etc. An ILF may be maintained by and counted as an ILF within more than one application; however, an ILF is counted only once per each application where it is maintained.

↩ An *elementary process* is the smallest unit of activity that is meaningful to the user. For example, a stock issue in a warehouse might be decomposed into various subprocesses such as Create, Read, Update, and Display (CRUD) so that the issue creates an amount due, reads a file to validate whether the individual has credit, and updates the quantity of stock on hand. The stock issue is the elementary process, not its subordinate subprocesses, and it may update more than one ILF through the same transaction.

All of the following IFPUG counting rules must apply for the data or control information to be counted as an ILF:

- The data or control information forms a logical, or user identifiable, group of data that fulfills specific user requirements.
- The group of data *is maintained within* the application boundary.
- The group of data is modified, or maintained, through an elementary process of the application.
- The group of data identified has not been counted as an EIF for the application.

Once a group of data has been identified as an ILF within an application, it can not also be counted as an EIF within the same application even if it is used for reference by other transactions, nor can it be counted as an EIF during an enhancement project for that application.

Some additional examples of internal logical files (ILFs) follow, but any group of data or control information must conform to the above definition and rules in order to be counted as ILFs:

◊ Application transaction data such as inventory issue records, employee training records, payroll records, credit card transactions, product sales, customer calls, accounts payable

◊ Application security or password data maintained within the application

◊ Audit data maintained within the application

◊ HELP data maintained within the application

◊ Edit data maintained within the application

◊ Parameter data maintained within the application

◊ Error files maintained within the application

◊ Mandatory back-up or historical data separately maintained within the application

The following examples of files, which have frequently been erroneously identified as ILFs, are provided (ensure that they are not counted as ILFs):

⊗ Temporary files or various iterations of the same file

⊗ Work files

⊗ Sort files

⊗ Extract files, or view files, which contain data extracted from other ILFs or EIFs prior to display or print

⊗ Files introduced because of technology

⊗ Alternative indices, joins, relationships or connections, unless they contain separately maintained non-key attributes

⊗ Files maintained by other applications and read or referenced only

⊗ Normal back-up data such as that used for corporate back-up and recovery

⊗ Suspense files containing incomplete transactions, which are not separately maintained

External Interface Files

An *external interface file (EIF)* is a user identifiable group of logically related data or control information referenced by the application but maintained within the boundary of a different application. The terms used in this definition are described below; they are very similar to the definitions provided earlier for ILFs:

↪ *User identifiable* refers to the specific requirements that an experienced user would define for the application, for example, a checking account record might be used for validation in an application that only reads the data while validating an unrelated transaction.

↪ *Logically related* refers to the requirement that each group should fit logically together within the descriptions provided. An EIF should not be dependent upon or attributive to another EIF in order to maintain its existence. Groups should be merged as necessary, particularly those that were created for performance or implementation reasons. EIFs are typically represented by entity types in second or third normal form. The data analysis equivalent to such high level logical groupings is a singular named data store on a data flow diagram, for example, an address table would probably belong to a higher level such as a client file, a billing file, an inventory location file, or an employee file.

↪ *Data* refers to the collection of facts and/or figures maintained within another application. For example, check number, amount, date, payee, memo entry, and account might be maintained in the checking account record for each check written.

↪ *Control information* is data used by the application to influence an elementary process of the application being counted. In the case of EIFs, these data, rules, or parameters are stored and maintained within a different application: for example, control data is maintained in Print Manager and read by Power-Point; edit data is referenced from another application in order to reject improper or inappropriate input data; dates and times are maintained by the users in one application so that they can be read or referenced within many different applications to establish the timing of events; certain thresholds are established to control an event in a different application such as setting the temperature on a thermostat which is then read by separate heating or air conditioning systems.

↪ *Maintained* refers to the fact that the data is created, modified, or deleted through an elementary process of another application. The data or control data could be maintained through such transactions as add, bill, change, delegate, evaluate, fail, grant, hold, populate, revise, update, etc. An EIF may be referenced by and counted as an EIF within more than one application; however, an EIF is counted only once per application.

All of the following IFPUG counting rules must apply for the data or control information to be counted as an EIF:

- The data or control information forms a logical, or user identifiable, group of data that fulfills specific user requirements.
- The group of data read or referenced is maintained external to the application being counted.
- The group of data is *not* maintained by the application being counted.
- The group of data identified has been counted as an ILF by at least one other application.
- The group of data identified has not been counted as an ILF by the application being counted.

Once a group of data has been identified as an EIF within an application, the EIF can not be counted again within the same application even if it is used for reference by other transactions or contains different data from the same file.

Some common examples of external interface files (EIFs) follow, but any group of data or control information must meet the previously given definition and rules in order to be counted as EIFs:

◊ Application data extracted and read from other applications

◊ Application security or password data maintained outside the application

◊ Audit data maintained outside the application

◊ HELP data maintained outside the application

◊ Edit data maintained outside the application

◊ Parameter data maintained outside the application

◊ Error files maintained outside the application

◊ Mandatory back-up or historical data separately maintained outside the application

The following examples of files, which have frequently been erroneously identified as EIFs, are provided (ensure that they are not counted as EIFs):

⊗ Data received from another application that maintains one or more ILFs within the application being counted (this is considered transactional data and should be counted as one or more external inputs)

⊗ Data maintained by the application being counted but accessed and used by a different application (this is counted as an ILF within the maintaining application and as an EIF to the accessing application)

⊗ Data formatted and sent by the application being counted to other applications (these should be counted as external outputs)

⊗ Temporary files or various iterations of the same file

⊗ Work files

⊗ Sort files

⊗ Extract files, or view files, that contain data extracted from previously counted EIFs prior to display or print

⊗ Files introduced because of technology

⊗ Alternative indices, joins, relationships, or connections, unless they contain separately maintained nonkey attributes

Complexity and Contribution—ILFs and EIFs. The number of ILFs and EIFs, together with the relative functional complexity for each, determine the contribution of the data function types to the Unadjusted Function Point count. Each identified ILF and EIF must be assigned a functional complexity based on the number of data element types (DETs) and record element types (RETs) associated with the ILF or EIF. Each of the terms used in the above definition are described below:

➥ *Functional complexity* is the rating assigned to each individual data function. Possible scores of low, average, and high are assigned using a complexity matrix which considers the number of DETs and RETs.

➥ *Data element types (DETs)* are unique user recognizable, nonrecursive fields/attributes, including foreign key attributes, maintained on the ILF or EIF.

↪ *Record element types (RETs)* are user recognizable subgroups (optional or mandatory) of data elements contained within an ILF or EIF. Subgroups are typically represented in an entity relationship diagram as entity subtypes or attributive entities, commonly called parent-child relationships. (The user has the option of using one or none of the optional subgroups during an elementary process that adds or creates an instance of the data; the user must use at least one of the mandatory subgroups.)

The following IFPUG rules apply when counting data elements/fields/attributes (termed DETs by IFPUG) for ILFs and EIFs:

- Count a DET for each unique user recognizable, nonrecursive field on the ILF or EIF; for example, check number, amount, date, payee, memo entry, and account number, maintained in the checking account record, would each count as one DET regardless of the number of checks written with unique data for each and regardless of how the data is physically stored.

- Count a DET for each field of data in an ILF or EIF that exists because the user requires that a relationship with another ILF be maintained; for example, a relationship exists to another ILF/EIF which requires a key with part number and location. These would be counted as two DETs unless, of course, either or both had been previously counted.

The following physical implementation techniques are counted as a single DET for the entire group of fields:

- • Fields that appear more than once in an ILF or EIF because of technology or implementation technique, such as the key mentioned above.

- • Repeating fields that are identical in format and exist to allow for multiple occurrences of a data value.

For example, an ILF containing twelve monthly amount fields and an annual total would be credited with two DETs, one for the repetitive monthly amounts and one to identify the total; one additional DET would undoubtedly be provided to identify the month (that is, Jan, Feb, etc).

The following IFPUG rules apply when counting record element types/subgroups of data elements within an ILF or EIF (termed RETs by IFPUG):

- Count a RET for each optional or mandatory subgroup of the ILF or EIF. Do not count any RETs that exist because of the technology or methodology utilized (that is, headers, trailers, separate text files, etc).

- If there are no subgroups, count the ILF or EIF as one RET.

An Example In Counting—ILFs and EIFs.   The user requirements for this example include the following:

△ The ability to maintain, inquire, and report employee information.

△ The location data for specific employees obtained from a file maintained by another application.

△ The ability to maintain, inquire, and report on information about jobs. (The user considers job description to be a collection of 80-character lines which describe the job; this information is not maintained independently from the job.)

△ The ability to maintain, inquire, and report on job assignments for employees.

△ The ability to inquire and report on different locations within the company, including a list of employees at a particular location; the location data is read only and is maintained by another application.

A process model for the user requirements might appear as follows:

EMPLOYEE MAINTENANCE
    CREATE EMPLOYEE
    EMPLOYEE INQUIRY
    UPDATE EMPLOYEE
    DELETE EMPLOYEE
    EMPLOYEE REPORT
JOB MAINTENANCE
    CREATE JOB
    JOB INQUIRY
    UPDATE JOB
    DELETE JOB
    JOB REPORT
JOB ASSIGNMENT MAINTENANCE
    ASSIGN EMPLOYEE TO JOB
    JOB ASSIGNMENT INQUIRY
    TRANSFER EMPLOYEE
    EVALUATE EMPLOYEE
    DELETE ASSIGNMENT
    JOB ASSIGNMENT REPORT
LOCATION REPORTING
    LOCATION INQUIRY
    LOCATION REPORT

An Entity Relationship Diagram might depict the data requirements as shown in Figure 4.1.

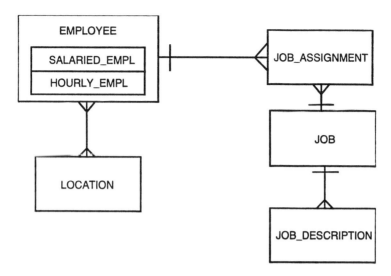

FIGURE 4.1   Entity Relationship Diagram for this Exercise

Various database structures could be utilized (Figure 4.2 A, B, C). This is not a book on databases, so forgive any author interpretation or misinterpretation. You don't need to understand any database methodology to count Function Points.

The fields contained in each of the entity types are listed below:

EMPLOYEE entity type
    Employee Name
    Social Security Number
    Nbr Dependents
    Type Code (Salaried or Hourly)
    Location Name (Foreign Key)
SALARIED EMPLOYEE entity subtype
    Supervisory Level
HOURLY EMPLOYEE entity subtype
    Standard Hourly Rate
    Collective Bargaining Unit Number
JOB entity type
    Job Name
    Job Number
    Pay Grade
JOB DESCRIPTION entity type (entity type for implementation process only, not a subgroup to users)

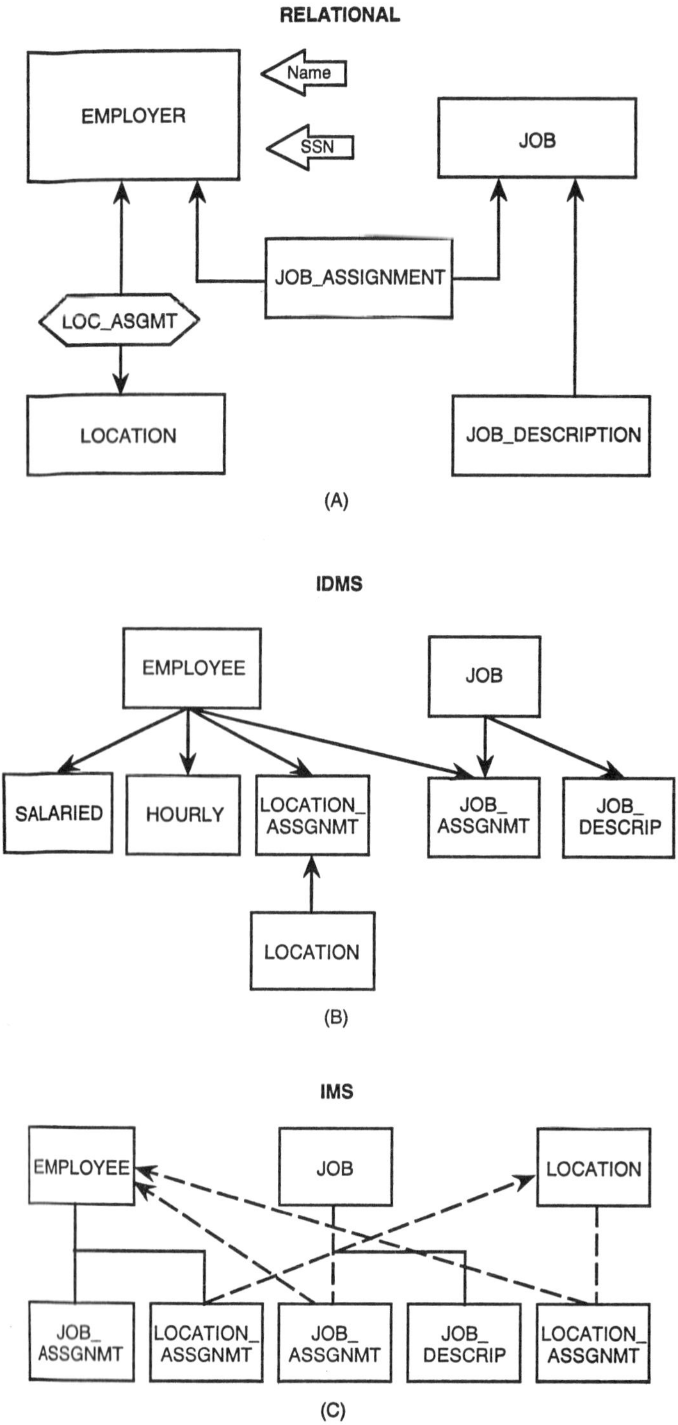

FIGURE 4.2 Potential Database Depictions of the Exercise

          Job Number (Foreign Key)
          Line Number (implementation process only; not significant to
            users)
          Description Line
     JOB ASSIGNMENT entity type
          Effective Date
          Salary
          Performance Rating
          Job Number (Foreign Key)
          Employee SSN (Foreign Key)
     LOCATION entity type
          Location Name
          Address
          Employee SSN (Foreign Key)

We will use this same model as we review the rules for transactional functions. It would be to the reader's benefit to review the above list and attempt to categorize the ILFs and EIFs with their DETs and RETs. We present the complexity matrix for ILFs/EIFs in Table 4.1 before providing the accurate count.

TABLE 4.1. Complexity Matrix for Internal Logical or External Interface Files

Record Element Types	Data Fields		
	1–19	20–50	51 +
<2	L	L	A
2–5	L	A	H
>5	A	H	H

And the answer is? If you followed all of the given information, lists, and fig ures, you had more detail than you might have in counting one of your own applications. Maybe there was too much. However, it is our view that you should have counted the following:

△ Employee as an ILF with 8 DETs and 2 RETs
△ Job as an ILF with 4 DETs and 1 RET
△ Job Assignment as an ILF with 5 DETs and 1 RET
△ Location as an EIF with 3 DETs and 1 RET

Let's go back and review those answers (Table 4.2).
     As Table 4.2 indicates, we end up with three low complexity ILFs and one low complexity EIF based on the complexity matrix for ILFs/EIFs. Most of our ac

TABLE 4.2   Identification of Files Included

File Fields	Counted As
EMPLOYEE entity type	A maintained ILF; not counted as a separate RET since there are subgroups
Employee Name	DET 1
Social Security Number	DET 2
Nbr Dependents	DET 3
Type Code (Salaried or Hourly)	DET 4
Location Name (Foreign Key)	DET 5
SALARIED EMPLOYEE entity subtype	RET 1 under Employee
Supervisory Level	DET 6
HOURLY EMPLOYEE entity subtype	RET 2 under Employee
Standard Hourly Rate	DET 7
Collective Bargaining Unit Number	DET 8
JOB entity type	A maintained ILF with 1 RET
Job Name	DET 1
Job Number	DET 2
Pay Grade	DET 3
JOB DESCRIPTION entity type	Exists for technological reasons only; part of Job
Job Number (Foreign Key)	Previously counted as DET 2
Line Number	Exists for technological reasons only
Description Line	DET 4
JOB ASSIGNMENT entity type	A maintained ILF with 1 RET; separately maintained with its own attributes
Effective Date	DET 1
Salary	DET 2
Performance Rating	DET 3
Job Number (Foreign Key)	DET 4
Employee SSN (Foreign Key)	DET 5
LOCATION entity type	A referenced EIF with 1 RET
Location Name	DET 1
Address	DET 2
Employee SSN (Foreign Key)	DET 3

tual files will be much larger, and we will have some average and high complexity files as well. So, what does all of this mean in terms of Function Points? Data transactions receive the highest weights/values when compared to transactional functions. The IFPUG Unadjusted Function Point Table is displayed in Table 4.3.

TABLE 4.3   IFPUG Unadjusted Function Points

Components	Function Levels		
	Low	Average	High
Internal Logical File (ILF)	X 7	X 10	X 15
External Interface File (EIF)	X 5	X 7	X 10
External Input (EI)	X 3	X 4	X 6
External Output (EO)	X 4	X 5	X 7
External Inquiry (EQ)	X 3	X 4	X 6

The ILFs contribute 21 and the EIF contributes 5 Unadjusted Function Points. We have addressed only the Unadjusted Function Point weights for ILFs/EIFs; we will cover the application characteristics adjustment (within step six) after we have covered transactional functions in the next chapter. We will provide some additional practical exercises later in the book to assist you in applying the IFPUG rules in counting data functions as well as transactional functions. The IFPUG *Counting Practices Manual* should be utilized to obtain the latest guidance on counting standards.

CHAPTER

5

TRANSACTIONAL
FUNCTION TYPES

INTRODUCTION

Information systems are usually developed with the intent that certain manual tasks can be accomplished more economically and effectively. It is these tasks that end up being identified as transactional functions. Let's assume we are running a catalog business. We currently process everything manually. We keep a file folder of descriptions for each item; we add items to that file folder, change descriptions when appropriate, and delete items from the folder when they are no longer available. When a customer calls and asks for a description, we retrieve it from the folder. Of course, we have other file folders as well: Some may contain inventory data and others may contain sales data. We produce a report at the end of the month that totals our sales for the month. The file folders that are available for update and retrieval are identified as internal logical files. Another file folder maintained elsewhere might contain vendor addresses to be categorized as an external interface file. In the last chapter we discussed these data function types. This chapter will describe the International Function Point User Group (IFPUG) definitions, rules, and guidelines for identifying transactional function types. The types include the following:

◊ External inputs, such as adding, changing, and deleting descriptions in our catalog example file folder

◊ External inquiries, such as the retrieval of a current description from our file folder

◊ External outputs, such as our report of monthly sales

More detailed guidance is contained within the IFPUG *Counting Practices Manual.* Later chapters will describe the General System Characteristics and the calculations involved in finalizing a Function Point count.

TRANSACTIONAL FUNCTION TYPES

The total process used to size Function Points was presented in previous chapters and is repeated here. The counting process can be summarized by the following seven steps:

1. Determine the type of Function Point count
2. Identify the application boundary
3. Identify all data functions and their complexity
4. Identify all transactional functions and their complexity*
5. Determine the Unadjusted Function Point count
6. Determine the Value Adjustment Factor—fourteen General System Characteristics
7. Calculate the final Adjusted Function Point Count

Remember that the application boundary separates the application being measured from the user domain and/or other independent applications. The data functions relate to the logical data stored and available for update and retrieval. The transactional functions, external inputs (EIs), external outputs (EOs) and external inquiries (EQs), perform the processes of updates, retrieval, outputs, etc. (transactions you would expect to see in a process model). Each has its own Unadjusted Function Point weight based upon its unique complexity matrix. First we will discuss external inputs followed by external outputs and external inquiries respectively.

External Inputs

An *external input (EI)* is an elementary process of the application which processes data or control information that enters from outside the boundary of the application.

---

*Discussed in this chapter

Processed data maintains one or more ILFs; processed control information may or may not maintain an ILF. The terms used in this definition are described below:

- ↪ An *elementary process* is the smallest unit of activity that is meaningful to the end-user in the business. This elementary process must be self-contained and leave the business of the application being counted in a consistent state; for example, an input form for health care coverage at a hospital could consist of three screens; however, if the form was incomplete until all three screens were completed, the elementary process would require the completion of all three screens. We would not question this decision if the form were to be completed manually; we would just hand it back to the individual and request that the entire form be completed. Completing some of the fields, even those on one screen, would neither be self-contained nor leave the business in a consistent state. If all information, recognizing that some of the fields may not be mandatory and could be left blank, is completed, this transaction would be complete, and the business would be left in a consistent state.

- ↪ *Data* refers to the facts and/or figures processed by the input transaction; for example, data would be the data fields included in the above health care transaction. We might expect to see patient name, name of the insured, date, time, medical problem, etc.

- ↪ *Control information* is data used by the application to influence an elementary process of the application being counted; in the case of EIs, these data, rules, or parameters may be saved/stored, or they may be used solely to maintain/initiate a process without being saved/stored after the process is complete. Control data, for example, is used to update/modify/maintain print manager; control data can also be entered within a different application such as Word without update capability. Control information is used by the application to ensure compliance with business function requirements specified by the user. It could include other features such as compare or calculate. In real-time systems, it may include incoming signals from an alarm, an instrument, a sensor, or another application.

- ↪ *Maintain* is the ability to create, modify, or delete data through an elementary process. Credit an EI for each data maintenance activity; for example, add, change, delete, populate, revise, update, assign, reset, save as, and create. There is practically no limit to the number of different verbs that might be chosen to maintain data.

There are separate sets of IFPUG rules that are applied to EI data transactions and control information.

All of the following counting rules must apply for the data being processed to be counted as an external input (EI):

- • The data must be received from outside the application boundary.
- • The data in at least one ILF must be maintained through an elementary process of the application.

- The process must be the smallest unit of activity that is meaningful to the end-user in the business.
- The process must be self-contained and leave the business of the application being counted in a consistent state.

For the identified process, either of the two following rules must apply:

1. Processing logic must be unique/different from other external inputs within the application. Processing logic is defined as any of the following requirements specifically requested by the user to complete an elementary process:
   Use of edits, algorithms, or calculations
   Reference to or use of an ILF or EIF
2. The data elements identified are different from other external inputs for the application.

All of the following counting rules must apply for the control information being processed to be counted as an external input (EI):

- The control information must be received from outside the application boundary.
- The control information must be specified by the user to ensure compliance with the business function requirements of the application.

For the identified process, either of the two following rules must apply:

1. Processing logic must be unique/different from other external inputs within the application. Processing logic is defined as any of the following requirements specifically requested by the user to complete an elementary process:
   Use of edits, algorithms, or calculations
   Reference to or use of an ILF or EIF
2. The data elements identified are different from other external inputs for the application. The processed control information may or may not maintain an ILF.

Some additional examples of External Inputs (EIs) follow, but any data or control information listed must conform to the above definition and rules in order to be counted as EIs:

◊ Transactional data that is used to maintain an ILF such as a sale, a receipt, an appointment, a transfer, etc.
◊ Screen input that maintains an ILF or provides control information
◊ Messages from other applications that require processing

◊ Transaction files from other applications (these may include multiple transactions of a different type which require separate and unique processing; for example, cash sales and credit card transactions in which case there would be multiple EIs)

◊ Batch input that maintains an ILF or provides control information

◊ User functions that either initiate control or enter data

◊ File of data maintained in prior application which must be processed through a conversion effort into a newly developed ILF when migrating data as part of a development or enhancement project; this would be included as part of the project count, but not within the application count

◊ Physical data that initiates processing

◊ Maintenance of any ILF, including HELP, any message file, parameters, etc.

The following examples of frequently misidentified EIs are provided (ensure that they are not counted as EIs):

⊗ Reference data which is read by the application from data stored in another application, but is not used to maintain an ILF in the counted application (counted as an EIF)

⊗ The input side of an inquiry

⊗ Menu screens used for navigation or selection and which do not maintain an ILF

⊗ Log-on screens that facilitate user entry into an application but do not maintain an ILF

⊗ Multiple methods of invoking same logic; for example, two action keys which perform the same function or the same transaction on multiple screens should be counted only once

⊗ Point and click of data on a screen in order to fill field(s) on the screen

⊗ Refresh or cancel screen data

⊗ Responses to messages that request a user to confirm a delete or any other transaction

⊗ Data passed between on-line and batch within the same application; it doesn't cross the boundary

⊗ Data passed between client and server within the same application; it doesn't cross the boundary

Complexity and Contribution—EIs. The *physical count* of EIs, together with the *relative functional complexity* for each, determine the contribution of the external inputs to the Unadjusted Function Point count. Each identified EI must be assigned a functional complexity based upon the number of data element types (DETs) and file types referenced (FTRs) associated with the EI. Each of the terms used in this definition are described below:

- ⇔ *Functional complexity* is the rating assigned to each individual transactional function. Possible scores of low, average, and high are assigned using a complexity matrix which considers the number of DETs and FTRs.
- ⇔ *Data element types (DETs)* are usually unique user recognizable, nonrecursive fields/attributes, including foreign key attributes, that cross the boundary of the application. Some other specific characteristics of a transaction, to be discussed later under rules, are also counted as DETs.
- ⇔ *File types referenced (FTRs),* or more simply files referenced, totals the number of internal logical files (ILFs) maintained, read, or referenced and the external interface files read or referenced by the EI transaction.

The following IFPUG rules apply when counting data elements/fields/attributes (termed DETs by IFPUG) for EIs:

- Count a DET for each unique user required, nonrecursive field/attribute, including foreign key attributes, that crosses the boundary of the application to complete the elementary process. Typically, they maintain an ILF; for example, item number, quantity sold, and date would each count as a DET on a sale transaction regardless of how the data is physically stored.
- Count a DET for each field that is not entered by the user but through an external input that is generated by the application and maintained on an internal logical file. A system generated date or account number are examples.

Count each of the following physical implementation techniques as a single DET for the entire group of fields:

- •• A logical field that is stored physically as multiple fields, but is required by the user as a single piece of information.
- •• Fields that appear more than once in an internal logical file because of technology or implementation techniques.
- •• Count a single DET to cover all the system responses which indicate an error occurred during processing or confirm that processing is complete.
- •• Count a single DET for the capability to specify the action to be taken by the external input. Count as one DET for each external input command lines or function/action (PF) keys that provide the capability to specify the action to be taken by the external input. Do not count a DET for each command function/action (PF) key.

The following IFPUG rules apply when counting file types referenced (termed FTRs by IFPUG):

- Count a file type referenced for each internal logical file (ILF) maintained.
- Count a file type referenced for each internal logical file (ILF) or external interface file (EIF) read during the processing of the external input.
- Count only one FTR for each ILF that is both maintained and read by the external input.

An Example in Counting EIs.   The user requirements discussed in the previous chapter include:

△ The ability to maintain, inquire, and report employee information. The report will include location data for specific employees obtained from a file maintained by another application.

△ The ability to maintain, inquire, and report on information about jobs. The user considers job description to be a collection of 80-character lines which describe the job; this information is not maintained independently from the job.

△ The ability to maintain, inquire, and report on job assignments for employees.

△ The ability to inquire and report on different locations within the company, including a list of employees at a particular location. The location data is read only and is maintained by another application.

A process model for the user requirements might appear as follows:

```
EMPLOYEE MAINTENANCE
    CREATE EMPLOYEE
    EMPLOYEE INQUIRY
    UPDATE EMPLOYEE
    DELETE EMPLOYEE
    EMPLOYEE REPORT
JOB MAINTENANCE
    CREATE JOB
    JOB INQUIRY
    UPDATE JOB
    DELETE JOB
    JOB REPORT
JOB ASSIGNMENT MAINTENANCE
    ASSIGN EMPLOYEE TO JOB
    JOB ASSIGNMENT INQUIRY
    TRANSFER EMPLOYEE
    EVALUATE EMPLOYEE
    DELETE ASSIGNMENT
    JOB ASSIGNMENT REPORT
```

LOCATION REPORTING
LOCATION INQUIRY
LOCATION REPORT

The internal logical files (ILFs) and external interface files were counted as shown in Table 5.1.

TABLE 5.1 Identification of Files Included

File/Fields	Counted As
EMPLOYEE entity type	A maintained ILF; not counted as a separate RET since there are subgroups
Employee Name	DET 1
Social Security Number	DET 2
Nbr Dependents	DET 3
Type Code (Salaried or Hourly)	DET 4
Location Name (Foreign Key)	DET 5
SALARIED EMPLOYEE entity subtype	RET 1 under Employee
Supervisory Level	DET 6
HOURLY EMPLOYEE entity subtype	RET 2 under Employee
Standard Hourly Rate	DET 7
Collective Bargaining Unit Number	DET 8
JOB entity type	A maintained ILF with 1 RET
Job Name	DET 1
Job Number	DET 2
Pay Grade	DET 3
JOB DESCRIPTION entity type	Exists for technological reasons only; part of Job
Job Number (Foreign Key)	Previously counted as DET 2
Line Number	Exists for technological reasons only
Description Line	DET 4
JOB ASSIGNMENT entity type	A maintained ILF with 1 RET; separately maintained with its own attributes
Effective Date	DET 1
Salary	DET 2
Performance Rating	DET 3
Job Number (Foreign Key)	DET 4
Employee SSN (Foreign Key)	DET 5
LOCATION entity type	A referenced EIF with 1 RET
Location Name	DET 1
Address	DET 2
Employee SSN (Foreign Key)	DET 3

Consequently, we counted three low complexity ILFs and one low complexity EIF based on the complexity matrix for ILFs/EIFs.

It would be to the reader's benefit to review Table 5.1 and attempt to identify the EIs with their DETs and FTRs. The complexity matrix for EIs is presented in Table 5.2.

TABLE 5.2.   Complexity Matrix for External Inputs

File Types Referenced	Data Fields		
	1–4	**5–15**	**16 +**
<2	L	L	A
2	L	A	H
>2	A	H	H

If you correctly identified only the EIs above, you would have counted ten EIs, which are listed in Table 5.3. We really don't have enough data to count the DETs and FTRs, but we can make a guess if we make a few assumptions. Let's assume that each input transaction returns error messages (we get a DET for each EI for that) and that each has at least one command key (we get another DET for each EI). Let's also assume that our create and update functions access all fields, but the delete functions touch only the primary key to that file. The assign and transfer functions should not touch the performance rating field, and the evaluate should not touch the salary field. Remember the extra two DETs for each transaction.

TABLE 5.3   Identification of External Inputs Included

EI Transactions	Counted As
EMPLOYEE MAINTENANCE	
CREATE EMPLOYEE	10 DETs and 2 FTRs, Employee and Location
UPDATE EMPLOYEE	10 DETs and 2 FTRs, Employee and Location
DELETE EMPLOYEE	3 DETs and 1 FTR, Employee
JOB MAINTENANCE	
CREATE JOB	6 DETs and 1 FTR, Job
UPDATE JOB	6 DETs and 1 FTR, Job
DELETE JOB	3 DETs and 1 FTR, Job
JOB ASSIGNMENT MAINTENANCE	
ASSIGN EMPLOYEE TO JOB	6 DETs and 3 FTRs, Employee, Job, and Job Assignment
TRANSFER EMPLOYEE	6 DETs and 3 FTRs, Employee, Job, and Job Assignment
EVALUATE EMPLOYEE	6 DETs and 1 FTR, Job Assignment
DELETE ASSIGNMENT	3 DETs and 1 FTR, Job Assignment

Calculating the complexities with that information, we would have six low complexity EIs, two average complexity EIs (create and update employee) and two high complexity EIs (assign and transfer employee). The IFPUG Unadjusted Function Point Table is displayed in Table 5.4. We would have a contribution of thirty-eight unadjusted Function Points for external inputs.

TABLE 5.4 IFPUG Unadjusted Function Points

	Function Levels		
Components	**Low**	**Average**	**High**
Internal Logical File (ILF)	X 7	X 10	X 15
External Interface File (EIF)	X 5	X 7	X 10
External Input (EI)	X 3	X 4	X 6
External Output (EO)	X 4	X 5	X 7
External Inquiry (EQ)	X 3	X 4	X 6

External Outputs

An *external output (EO)* is an elementary process of the application which generates data or control information that exits the boundary of the application. The terms used in this definition are described below:

- ↪ An *elementary process* is the smallest unit of activity that is meaningful to the end-user in the business. This elementary process must be self-contained and leave the business of the application being counted in a consistent state. For example, a report may consist of numerous pages, but if the pages are not independently required and produced, it is only one EO. Producing some of the fields (even one page) would neither be self-contained nor leave the business in a consistent state. If all information, recognizing that some of the fields may not be filled and could be left null or blank, is completed, this transaction would be complete, and the business would be left in a consistent state.

- ↪ *Data* refers to the facts and/or figures processed by the output transaction. For example, data would be the data fields included in the report transaction example. We might expect to see fields such as department name, department number, address, month, monthly sales, monthly purchases, current running total for the year, etc.

- ↪ *Control information* is data used by the application to influence an elementary process of the application being counted. In the case of EOs, these data, rules, or parameters may be sent by the application to a user or to another application; for example, control information could be sent by the application to ensure compliance with business function requirements specified by the user. It could include messages to the user advising that certain parameter dates or times had been reached such as an alarm or screen notification of an appointment or a meeting or a due date. In real-time systems, it may include outgoing signals such as an alarm, a message, or shutdown of a manufacturing line.

All of the following counting rules must apply for the data being processed to be counted as an external output (EO):

- The data or control information must be sent outside the application boundary.
- The data or control information must be sent through an elementary process of the application.
- The process must be the smallest unit of activity that is meaningful to the end user in the business.
- The process must be self-contained and leave the business of the application being counted in a consistent state.

For the identified process, either of the two following rules must apply:

1. Processing logic must be unique/different from other external outputs within the application. Processing logic is defined as any of the following requirements specifically requested by the user to complete an elementary process:

    Use of edits, algorithms, or calculations
    Reference to or use of an ILF or EIF

    Rearranging, reformatting, or resorting a set of data is not considered to be unique processing logic; however, there may be other unique processing logic when this occurs. As an example, a report with totals could be available with sorts by month, product, and department. If the report fields are the same (even if displayed in a different format), the totals are by column, and the processing calculations are not unique, we would count one EO. Three EOs would be counted if the totals are summarized differently and the calculations are unique for each different sort. Perhaps, there would be internal totals displaying totals of a product by month within a department, monthly totals of a department by division, and product sales by days of the month.

2. The data elements identified are different from other external outputs for the application. Note that these are different data elements and not different data in the same fields. For example, account statements produced for individuals that have different data in the same fields are counted as one EO. Two separately produced reports at the detail and summary levels would be counted as two EOs because of the unique processing logic and calculations.

Some additional examples of External Outputs (EOs) follow, but any data or control information listed below must meet the above definition and rules in order to be counted as EOs:

◊ Reports that require the use of algorithms or calculations; for example, monthly checking account statements or weekly sales reports

◊ Data transfers, files, and/or messages sent to other applications; for example, a file of transactions sent from the accounts receivable application to the separately maintained general ledger application (an EO to accounts receivables and one or more EIs to general ledger)

◊ Multiple data files, each produced through a separate and distinct elementary process, sent to another application

◊ A conversion report that reports the result of the conversion effort when migrating data as part of a development or enhancement project; this would be included as part of the project count, but not within the application count

◊ Informational messages other than error reports or confirmation messages

◊ Derived/calculated information displayed on a screen

◊ Graphical displays such as bar charts and pie charts

◊ Bar coded labels

◊ Calculated responses returned by telephone

◊ Microfiche history report

◊ Payroll checks; another EO would be counted for documents produced for direct deposit

◊ A calculated firing solution, returned to the user or sent to another application within the weapon system, for a weapon

◊ Notification that a credit card has been reported missing

◊ Calculation of a proposed premium on an insurance policy

The following examples of frequently misidentified EOs are provided (ensure that they are not counted as EOs):

⊗ Identical reports with different data values, such as a department report (counted only once)

⊗ Summary fields contained on a detail report (counted together as one EO)

⊗ Refresh or cancel screen data

⊗ Resorting or rearrangement of a set of data without other processing logic

⊗ Reference data that is read by another application from data stored in the application being counted (the data is not processed as an output by the counted application)

⊗ The output side of an inquiry

⊗ Help (counted as an EQ)

⊗ Log-off

⊗ Multiple methods of invoking the same output process

⊗ Error messages that result from an edit or validation of an EI or the input side of an EQ

⊗ Confirmation messages that acknowledge that the data has been processed

⊗ Messages that request a user to confirm a delete or any other transaction

⊗ Identical data sent to more than one application (counted only once)

⊗ Ad-hoc reports which the user directs and controls often through the use of a language such as SQL or FOCUS

⊗ Data passed between on-line and batch within the same application; it doesn't cross the boundary

⊗ Data passed between client and server within the same application; it doesn't cross the boundary

Complexity and Contribution—EOs. The *physical count* of EOs, together with the *relative functional complexity* for each, determine the contribution of the external outputs to the Unadjusted Function Point count. Each identified EO must be assigned a functional complexity based on the number of data element types (DETs) and file types referenced (FTRs) associated with the EO. The terms used in this definition are described below:

↬ *Functional complexity* is the rating assigned to each individual transactional function. Possible scores of low, average, and high are assigned using a complexity matrix which considers the number of DETs and FTRs.

↬ *Data element types (DETs)* are unique, user recognizable, nonrecursive fields/attributes that leave the boundary of the application.

↬ *File types referenced (FTRs),* or more simply files referenced, totals the number of internal logical files (ILFs) read or referenced and the external interface files read or referenced by the EO transaction.

The following IFPUG rules apply when counting data elements/fields/attributes (termed DETs by IFPUG) for EOs:

• Count a DET for each unique, user required, nonrecursive field/attribute that appears on the EO. This includes unique data fields or control information.

• Do not count paging variable or system-generated stamps including page numbers, positioning information (row x of y), paging commands (previous, next, arrows), or date/time fields.

• Do not count literals, including report titles, screen IDs, column headings, or field titles.

Count the following physical implementation techniques as a single DET for the entire group of fields:

•• A logical field that is stored physically as multiple fields, but is required by the user as a single piece of information; for example, a date or name stored as three fields but used as one field is counted as one DET.

•• Each type of label and each type of numerical equivalent in a graphical display; for example, a pie chart might have two DETs, one for the category and one for the applicable percentage.

•• Text information that may consist of a single word, a sentence, a paragraph, or many paragraphs.

The following IFPUG rule applies when counting file types referenced (termed FTRs by IFPUG):

• Count a file type referenced for each internal logical file (ILF) or external interface file (EIF) read during the processing of the external output.

An Example in Counting EOs.   The user requirements discussed in the previous chapter include the following:

△ The ability to maintain, inquire, and report employee information. The report will include location data for specific employees obtained from a file maintained by another application.

△ The ability to maintain, inquire, and report on information about jobs. The user considers job description to be a collection of 80-character lines which describe the job; this information is not maintained independently from the job.

△ The ability to maintain, inquire, and report on job assignments for employees.

△ The ability to inquire and report on different locations within the company, including a list of employees at a particular location. The location data is read only and is maintained by another application.

A process model for the user requirements might appear as follows:

```
EMPLOYEE MAINTENANCE
    CREATE EMPLOYEE
    EMPLOYEE INQUIRY
    UPDATE EMPLOYEE
    DELETE EMPLOYEE
    EMPLOYEE REPORT
JOB MAINTENANCE
    CREATE JOB
    JOB INQUIRY
    UPDATE JOB
```

DELETE JOB
JOB REPORT
JOB ASSIGNMENT MAINTENANCE
ASSIGN EMPLOYEE TO JOB
JOB ASSIGNMENT INQUIRY
TRANSFER EMPLOYEE
EVALUATE EMPLOYEE
DELETE ASSIGNMENT
JOB ASSIGNMENT REPORT
LOCATION REPORTING
LOCATION INQUIRY
LOCATION REPORT

The internal logical files (ILFs) and external interface files were counted as shown in Table 5.5. We counted three low complexity ILFs and one low complexity EIF based upon the complexity matrix for ILFs/EIFs. It would be to the reader's benefit to review Table 5.5 and attempt to identify the EOs with their FTRs. There is not enough information to count the DETs. In fact, there really isn't enough information to distinguish the EOs from the EQs. Let's assume that each of the reports contains derived or calculated data and that all inquiries will be counted as EQs. Let's also assume that each of the reports, except the job report, has between six and nineteen DETs, and that the job report has five DETs. In fact when we determine the complexities of any transaction, we need to know only DETs within a particular range based on the complexity matrix for that particular transaction. Note that the applicable ranges for DETs on EOs equate to less than six, six to nineteen, and more than nineteen. We can usually make a good guess at that before we get to design.

TABLE 5.5   Identification of Files Included

File/Fields	Counted As
EMPLOYEE entity type	A maintained ILF; not counted as a separate RET since there are subgroups
Employee Name	DET 1
Social Security Number	DET 2
Nbr Dependents	DET 3
Type Code (Salaried or Hourly)	DET 4
Location Name (Foreign Key)	DET 5
SALARIED EMPLOYEE entity subtype	RET 1 under Employee
Supervisory Level	DET 6

TABLE 5.5 Continued

File/Fields	Counted As
HOURLY EMPLOYEE entity subtype	RET 2 under Employee
Standard Hourly Rate	DET 7
Collective Bargaining Unit Number	DET 8
JOB entity type	A maintained ILF with 1 RET
Job Name	DET 1
Job Number	DET 2
Pay Grade	DET 3
JOB DESCRIPTION entity type	Exists for technological reasons only; part of Job
Job Number (Foreign Key)	Previously counted as DET 2
Line Number	Exists for technological reasons only
Description Line	DET 4
JOB ASSIGNMENT entity type	A maintained ILF with 1 RET; separately maintained with its own attributes
Effective Date	DET 1
Salary	DET 2
Performance Rating	DET 3
Job Number (Foreign Key)	DET 4
Employee SSN (Foreign Key)	DET 5
LOCATION entity type	A referenced EIF with 1 RET
Location Name	DET 1
Address	DET 2
Employee SSN (Foreign Key)	DET 3

TABLE 5.6. Complexity Matrix for External Outputs

File Types Referenced	Data Fields		
	1–5	6–19	20 +
<2	L	L	A
2–3	L	A	H
>3	A	H	H

The complexity matrix for EOs is presented in Table 5.6. You should be able to count four EOs; that was not very difficult. Counting EOs is usually not difficult, particularly when you have knowledge of the system to be counted. The EOs are listed here:

EMPLOYEE MAINTENANCE
    EMPLOYEE REPORT
JOB MAINTENANCE
    JOB REPORT
JOB ASSIGNMENT MAINTENANCE
    JOB ASSIGNMENT REPORT
LOCATION REPORTING
    LOCATION REPORT

O.K., how many FTRs? I didn't say this was easy. If we had a user or developer, we could ask. If we had a copy of the reports, we could search our ILFs for the fields contained. The employee report would obviously reference the employee file and might also reference the location file, since there is a relationship between the two files. With two FTRs and six to nineteen DETs, the EO would be average.

The job report contains five DETs (that was given) and probably only one FTR, the job file. Consequently, it would equate to a low EO. The job assignment report, with six to nineteen DETs, could have three FTRs, job assignment, employee, and job. With three FTRs, it is an average EO. Finally, the location report must reference two FTRs; how else could it contain at least six DETs. Let's guess it to be average. That equates to three average EOs and one low EO.

The IFPUG Unadjusted Function Point Table is displayed in Table 5.7. From the table we see that the external outputs provide a contribution of nineteen Unadjusted Function Points.

TABLE 5.7   IFPUG Unadjusted Function Points

Components	Function Levels		
	Low	Average	High
Internal Logical File (ILF)	X 7	X 10	X 15
External Interface File (EIF)	X 5	X 7	X 10
External Input (EI)	X 3	X 4	X 6
External Output (EO)	X 4	X 5	X 7
External Inquiry (EQ)	X 3	X 4	X 6

External Inquiries

An *external inquiry (EQ)* is an elementary process of the application which is made up of an input-output combination that results in data retrieval. The input side is the control information which spells out the request, specifying what and/or how data is to be retrieved. The output side contains no derived data. No ILF is maintained during processing. The terms used in this definition are described below:

↪ An *elementary process* is the smallest unit of activity that is meaningful to the end-user in the business. This elementary process must be self-contained and leave the business of the application being counted in a consistent state. In order to perform, for example, a particular retrieval of data, the users have requested they be able to enter up to five different fields of control information; for example, model, color, style, year manufactured, and warranty. Any number of combinations would be possible, but each of the five can be selected as an and/or selection. Entering one of the fields would not be an elementary process; neither would entering all five. Possible candidates fulfilling the criteria of the control information entered must first be extracted and presented to the requester before the transaction would be considered to be an elementary process. An EQ involves a request for display, an extract of what is to be displayed, and the display itself; without all three subactivities the transaction is not complete.

↪ *Control information* is data used by the application to influence an elementary process of the application being counted. In the case of EQs, these data, rules, or parameters specify what and/or how the data is to be retrieved. The control information is not an elementary process on its own.

↪ *Derived data* requires processing, other than direct retrieval and editing of information, from one or more ILFs and/or EIFs. The most common are calculations or totals.

↪ *Maintain* is the ability to create, modify, or delete data through an elementary process. An EQ does not maintain data; an EI maintains data. It is possible that an EI could occur simultaneously with an EQ, but they both would be independent elementary processes. For example, information could be saved regarding particular user retrievals, such as sensitive or classified information.

All of the following counting rules must apply for the data being processed to be counted as an external inquiry (EQ):

- The input request must be received from outside the application boundary.
- The output results must exit the application boundary.
- Data must be retrieved from one or more ILFs/EIFs.
- The retrieved and displayed data must not contain derived data.

- The input request, retrieval, and output result together make up a process that is the smallest unit of activity that is meaningful to the end user in the business.
- The process must be self-contained and leave the business of the application being counted in a consistent state.
- The process does not update an ILF.

For the identified process, either of the two following rules must apply:

1. Processing logic on the input or output side must be unique/different from other external inquiries within the application. Processing logic is defined as any of the following requirements specifically requested by the user to complete an elementary process:
   Use of edits
   Reference to or use of an ILF or EIF
2. The data elements making up the input or output side are different from other external inquiries within the application.

Some additional examples of External Inquiries (EQs) follow, but any examples listed below must conform to the above definition and rules in order to be counted as EQs:

◊ Transactional data that is retrieved, from one or more ILFs and/or EIFs, and displayed based upon input criteria; for example, an appointment, an item description, employee data, payment data, etc.
◊ User functions such as view, lookup, display, browse
◊ Implied inquiries (retrievals of data prior to a change or delete function), provided that the inquiry can be used as a stand-alone process and that it is not a duplication of another previously counted EQ
◊ Maintained system data, parameters, and setup unless computed
◊ Logon screens that provide application specific security
◊ Each level of Help; for example, system, field, or screen, counted once per level per application
◊ Retrievals of maintained data via electronic data interface or phone (using tones)
◊ Retrieval of mail from mailbox
◊ List boxes or point and click on a screen in order to return maintained data

The following examples of frequently misidentified EQs are provided (ensure that they are not counted as EQs):

⊗ Multiple methods of invoking same logic; for example, two action keys which perform the same function or the same transaction on multiple screens should be counted only once

⊗ Inquiries that can be accessed from multiple areas/screens of an application (count once)

⊗ Menu screens used for navigation or selection and which do not retrieve maintained data

⊗ Log on screens that facilitate user entry into an application but do not invoke security

⊗ Derived data versus retrieval of data (counted as an EO)

⊗ Resorting or rearrangement of a set of data without other processing logic

⊗ Responses to messages that request a user to confirm data

⊗ Error and/or confirmation messages

⊗ On-line system documentation

⊗ Data passed between on-line and batch within the same application; it doesn't cross the boundary

⊗ Data passed between client and server within the same application; it doesn't cross the boundary

⊗ Data which is not retrieved from maintained data; for example, hard coded data

Complexity and Contribution—EQs. The *physical count* of EQs, together with the *relative functional complexity* for each, determine the contribution of the external inquiries to the unadjusted Function Point count. Each identified EQ must be assigned a functional complexity based upon the number of data element types (DETs) and file types referenced (FTRs) associated with both the input and output sides of the EQ. The higher of the two complexities (from the input and output sides of the inquiry) is used as the complexity for the EQ. The terms used in this definition are described below:

↪ *Functional complexity* is the rating assigned to each individual transactional function. Possible scores of low, average, and high are assigned to EQs using the same two complexity matrices, which are used for EIs and EOs, by considering the number of DETs and FTRs.

↪ *Data element types (DETs)* are unique, user recognizable, nonrecursive fields/attributes, that appear in the EQ and cross the boundary of the application. Some other specific characteristics of DETs for EQs will be discussed later under rules.

↪ *File types referenced (FTRs),* or more simply files referenced, totals the number of internal logical files (ILFs) and external interface files read or referenced by the EQ transaction.

The following IFPUG rules apply when counting data elements/fields/attributes (termed DETs by IFPUG) for the input side of EQs:

- Count a DET for each unique user required, nonrecursive field/attribute, including foreign key attributes and control information, that crosses the boundary of the application, on the input side of an inquiry.
- Count a DET for each field that specifies the data selection criteria.
- Count each of the following physical implementation techniques as a single DET for the entire group of fields:
  - •• Count a single DET to cover all the system responses that indicate an error occurred during processing or confirm that processing is complete.
  - •• Count a single DET for the capability to specify that the external inquiry is to be executed.
  - •• Count a single DET for command lines or function/action (PF) keys that provide the capability to specify the action to be taken. Do not count it per command function/action (PF) key.

The following IFPUG rules apply when counting data elements/fields/attributes (termed DETs by IFPUG) for the output side of EQs:

- Count a DET for each unique, user required, nonrecursive field/attribute, including foreign key attributes and control information, that crosses the boundary of the application and appears on the output side of the inquiry. This includes unique data fields or control information.
- Do not count paging variable or system-generated stamps including page numbers, positioning information (row x of y), paging commands (previous, next, arrows), or date/time fields.
- Do not count literals, including report titles, screen IDs, column headings, or field titles.

Count the following physical implementation techniques as a single DET for the entire group of fields:

- •• A logical field that is stored physically as multiple fields, but is required by the user as a single piece of information.
- •• Fields that appear more than once in an internal logical file because of technology or implementation techniques.
- •• Each type of label and each type of numerical equivalent in a graphical display; this would be restricted to maintained data, not derived data.

The following IFPUG rule applies when counting file types referenced (termed FTRs by IFPUG):

- Count a file type referenced for each internal logical file (ILF) or external interface file (EIF) read during the processing of the external inquiry. This same rule applies to both the input and output sides of the external inquiry.

An Example in Counting EQs.   The user requirements discussed previously include the following:

△ The ability to maintain, inquire, and report employee information—the report will include location data for specific employees obtained from a file maintained by another application

△ The ability to maintain, inquire, and report on information about jobs—the user considers job description to be a collection of 80-character lines which describe the job; this information is not maintained independently from the job

△ The ability to maintain, inquire, and report on job assignments for employees

△ The ability to inquire and report on different locations within the company, including the ability to generate a list of employees at a particular location— the location data is read only and is maintained by another application

A process model for the user requirements might appear as follows:

```
EMPLOYEE MAINTENANCE
       CREATE EMPLOYEE
       EMPLOYEE INQUIRY
       UPDATE EMPLOYEE
       DELETE EMPLOYEE
       EMPLOYEE REPORT
JOB MAINTENANCE
       CREATE JOB
       JOB INQUIRY
       UPDATE JOB
       DELETE JOB
       JOB REPORT
JOB ASSIGNMENT MAINTENANCE
       ASSIGN EMPLOYEE TO JOB
       JOB ASSIGNMENT INQUIRY
       TRANSFER EMPLOYEE
       EVALUATE EMPLOYEE
       DELETE ASSIGNMENT
       JOB ASSIGNMENT REPORT
LOCATION REPORTING
       LOCATION INQUIRY
       LOCATION REPORT
```

The internal logical files (ILFs) and external interface files (EIFs) were counted as shown in Table 5.8. It would be to the reader's benefit to quickly review Table 5.8. Since we have already identified the EIs and EOs, only the EQs remain. Their DETs and RETs are not obvious, so it is important to know that an EQ requires entry of

TABLE 5.8   Identification of Files Included

File/Fields	Counted As
EMPLOYEE entity type	A maintained ILF; not counted as a separate RET since there are subgroups
Employee Name	DET 1
Social Security Number	DET 2
Nbr Dependents	DET 3
Type Code (Salaried or Hourly)	DET 4
Location Name (Foreign Key)	DET 5
SALARIED EMPLOYEE entity subtype	RET 1 under Employee
Supervisory Level	DET 6
HOURLY EMPLOYEE entity subtype	RET 2 under Employee
Standard Hourly Rate	DET 7
Collective Bargaining Unit Number	DET 8
JOB entity type	A maintained ILF with 1 RET
Job Name	DET 1
Job Number	DET 2
Pay Grade	DET 3
JOB DESCRIPTION entity type	Exists for technological reasons only; part of Job
Job Number (Foreign Key)	Previously counted as DET 2
Line Number	Exists for technological reasons only
Description Line	DET 4
JOB ASSIGNMENT entity type	A maintained ILF with 1 RET; separately maintained with its own attributes
Effective Date	DET 1
Salary	DET 2
Performance Rating	DET 3
Job Number (Foreign Key)	DET 4
Employee SSN (Foreign Key)	DET 5
LOCATION entity type	A referenced EIF with 1 RET
Location Name	DET 1
Address	DET 2
Employee SSN (Foreign Key)	DET 3

only those fields and control information necessary to accomplish the retrieval of the data. Lets assume for this exercise that the control information for each is either one or two fields. In addition, the input side of each inquiry transaction returns error messages (we get a DET on the input side for that) and has at least one command key (we get another DET on the input side for each EQ).

In this, as in most cases, the FTRs are the same on both sides. The one major exception would be a maintained error message file which is referenced on the input side of an EQ but not the output side. We did not have such a file, because we did not have an ILF or EIF for error messages. The FTRs for both the input and output sides, and the DETs for the output sides, for each of the EQs are as follows:

EMPLOYEE INQUIRY: 2 FTRs and 9 DETs (output side)
JOB INQUIRY: 1 FTR and 4 DETs (output side)
JOB ASSIGNMENT INQUIRY: 1 FTR and 5 DETs (output side)
LOCATION INQUIRY: 2 FTRs and 5 DETs (output side)

You might ask why there is only one file referenced on the job assignment EQ. We do not need to reference the employee or job file for validation, and none of those fields were retrieved. The complexity matrices for EQs uses the EI matrix for the input side of the EQ and the EO matrix for the output side of the EQ. Both matrices were previously presented, but they are presented again in Tables 5.9 and 5.10.

TABLE 5.9. Complexity Matrix for Input Side of External Inquiries

File Types Referenced	Data Fields		
	1–4	5–15	16 +
<2	L	L	A
2	L	A	H
>2	A	H	H

TABLE 5.10. Complexity Matrix for Output Side of External Inquiries

File Types Referenced	Data Fields		
	1–5	6–19	20 +
<2	L	L	A
2–3	L	A	H
>3	A	H	H

Calculating the complexities with the information from the tables, we would have three low complexity EQs (job, job-assignment, and location) and one average complexity EQ (employee). Table 5.11 is the IFPUG Unadjusted Function Point Table and shows that we would have a contribution of thirteen Function Points for external inquires. The IFPUG *Counting Practices Manual* should be utilized to obtain the latest guidance on counting standards.

TABLE 5.11   IFPUG Unadjusted Function Points

Components	Function Levels		
	Low	Average	High
Internal Logical File (ILF)	X 7	X 10	X 15
External Interface File (EIF)	X 5	X 7	X 10
External Input (EI)	X 3	X 4	X 6
External Output (EO)	X 4	X 5	X 7
External Inquiry (EQ)	X 3	X 4	X 6

CHAPTER

6

GENERAL SYSTEM CHARACTERISTICS

INTRODUCTION

The user/owner function delivered by information systems includes pervasive general factors that are not sufficiently represented by the countable transactional and data functions. This chapter will describe the International Function Point User Group (IFPUG) definitions, rules, and guidelines for identifying the Value Adjustment Factor (VAF), which is used as a multiplier of the Unadjusted Function Point Count in order to calculate the Final Adjusted Function Point Count of an application. The VAF is calculated based on the identification of fourteen General System Characteristics (GSCs). They include the following:

1. Data Communications
2. Distributed Data Processing
3. Performance
4. Heavily Used Configuration
5. Transaction Rate
6. On-Line Data Entry

   7. End-User Efficiency
   8. On-Line Update
   9. Complex Processing
   10. Reusability
   11. Installation Ease
   12. Operational Ease
   13. Multiple Sites
   14. Facilitate Change

   Detailed guidance is contained within the IFPUG *Counting Practices Manual.* The following chapter will utilize the results of the identification of data and transactional function types as well as the values obtained from identifying the GSCs to calculate a final Function Point count.

THE FUNCTION POINT PROCESS

The total process used to size Function Points was presented in previous chapters and is repeated here. The counting process can be summarized by the following seven steps:

   1. Determine the type of Function Point count
   2. Identify the application boundary
   3. Identify all data functions and their complexity
   4. Identify all transactional functions and their complexity
   5. Determine the Unadjusted Function Point count*
   6. Determine the Value Adjustment Factor—fourteen General System Characteristics*
   7. Calculate the final Adjusted Function Point Count

Remember that the application boundary separates the application being measured from the user domain and/or other independent applications. The data functions relate to the logical data stored and available for update and retrieval. The transactional functions, external inputs (EIs), external outputs (EOs), and external inquiries (EQs), perform the processes of updates, retrieval, outputs, etc. (transactions you would expect to see in a process model). Each has its own unadjusted function point weight based on its unique complexity matrix. The General System Characteristics (GSCs) will each be evaluated independently and assigned a unique value between zero (0) and five (5). These scores will be summed to calculate a Total Degree of Influence. Then, the Total Degree of Influence will be used in a separate calculation to determine the Value Adjustment Factor (VAF).

   *Discussed in this chapter

GENERAL SYSTEM CHARACTERISTICS

Each General System Characteristic (GSC) must be evaluated in terms of its Degree of Influence (DI) on a scale of zero to five:

0   Not present, or no influence
1   Incidental influence
2   Moderate influence
3   Average influence
4   Significant influence
5   Strong influence throughout

There are IFPUG guidelines for assigning the Degree of Influence (DI) for each General System Characteristic (GSC). The remainder of this chapter will provide the IFPUG guidelines for assigning values to each of the fourteen GSCs. Additionally, the authors' comments will assist in assigning these values to different types of applications. If none of the IFPUG guideline descriptions fit the application exactly, a judgment must be made about which Degree of Influence (DI) most closely applies to the application. Our discussion of the fourteen GSCs follows.

1. Data Communication. The *data* and *control* information used in the application are sent or received over communication facilities. Terminals connected locally to the control unit are considered to use communication facilities. Protocol is a set of conventions which permit the transfer or exchange of information between two systems or devices. All data communication links require some type of protocol. Score as follows:

0   Application is pure batch processing or a stand alone PC.
1   Application is batch but has remote data entry or remote printing.
2   Application is batch but has remote data entry and remote printing.
3   On-line data collection or TP (teleprocessing) front end to a batch process or query system.
4   More than a front-end, but the application supports only one type of TP communications protocol.
5   More than a front-end, but the application supports more than one type of TP communications protocol.

Authors' notes: We would expect only batch applications with no interactivity to be valued at zero. Most applications, stand-alone PC, as well as batch, have remote data entry as well as printing capability. Those applications that have front end data entry screens, but which update internal logical files through a batch process, should be scored at three. If update occurs immediately, score four. In order to score five, there must be multiple types of telecommunication protocol. Typically, batch receives a score of zero to three; on-line scores a three to a four; real-time, telecommunication, or process control systems receive a score of four or five.

2. Distributed Data Processing. Distributed data or processing functions are a characteristic of the application within the application boundary. Score as follows:

0   Application does not aid the transfer of data or processing function between components of the system.

1   Application prepares data for end-user processing on another component of the system such as PC spreadsheets and PC DBMS.

2   Data is prepared for transfer, transferred, and processed on another component of the system (not for end-user processing).

3   Distributed processing and data transfer are on-line and in one direction only.

4   Distributed processing and data transfer are on-line and in both directions.

5   Processing functions are dynamically performed on the most appropriate component of the system.

Authors' notes: Only distributed or real-time applications would be assigned a value within this category. Most applications score zero; primative distributed applications could score one or two; client server scores a two to a four; real-time, telecommunication, or process control systems could score zero through five. In order to score a five there must be multiple servers or processors.

3. Performance. Application performance objectives, stated or approved by the user, in either response or throughput, influenced (or will influence) the design, development, installation, and support of the application. Score as follows:

0   No special performance requirements were stated by the user.

1   Performance and design requirements were stated and reviewed but no special actions were required.

2   Response time or throughput is critical during peak hours. No special design for CPU utilization was required. Processing deadline is for the next business day.

3   Response time or throughput is critical during all business hours. No special design for CPU utilization was required. Processing deadline requirements with interfacing systems are constraining.

4   Stated user performance requirements are stringent enough to require performance analysis tasks in the design phase.

5   In addition, performance analysis tools were used in the design, develop-

ment, and/or implementation phases to meet the stated user performance requirements.

Authors' notes: GSC 3 and GSC 5 are very similar in nature; both require consideration of performance during the design, development, and installation phases of development. Response time typically relates to interactive processing; throughput relates to batch processing. Consider the significance of performance to the particular application. A score of four requires performance analysis tasks during the design phase. A score of five requires the use of performance analysis tools. Typically, batch receives a score of zero to four; on-line scores zero to four; real-time, telecommunication, or process control systems score zero to five.

4. Heavily Used Configuration. A heavily used operational configuration, requiring special design considerations, is a characteristic of the application; for example, the user wants to run the application on existing or committed equipment that will be heavily used. Score as follows:

0 There are no explicit or implicit operational restrictions.
1 Operational restrictions do exist, but are less restrictive than a typical application. No special effect is needed to meet the restrictions.
2 Some security or timing considerations exist.
3 There are specific processor requirements for a specific piece of the application.
4 Stated operation restrictions require special constraints on the application in the central processor or a dedicated processor.
5 In addition, there are special constraints on the application in the distributed components of the system.

Authors' notes: We would expect most applications to be valued at two. In order to score three through five, you would expect to have a client server, real-time, telecommunication, or process control systems. Even then, you would need either a dedicated processor or multiple processors processing the same transactions and searching for the most expeditious means of processing.

5. Transaction Rate. The transaction rate is high and it influenced the design, development, installation, and support of the application. Score as follows:

0 No peak transaction period is anticipated.
1 A peak transaction period (monthly, quarterly, seasonally, annually) is anticipated.
2 A weekly peak transaction period is anticipated.
3 A daily peak transaction period is anticipated.

4   High transaction rates stated by the user in the application requirements or service level agreements are high enough to require performance analysis tasks in the design phase.

5   High transaction rates stated by the user in the application requirements or service level agreements are high enough to require performance analysis tasks and, in addition, require the use of performance analysis tools in the design, development, and/or installation phases.

Authors' notes: GSC 3 and GSC 5 are very similar in nature; both require consideration of performance during the design, development, and installation phases of development. Consider the significance of transaction rates to the particular application. A score of four requires performance analysis tasks during the design phase. A score of five requires the use of performance analysis tools. Typically, batch receives a score of zero to three; on-line scores zero to four; real-time, telecommunication, or process control systems score zero to five.

   6. On-line Data Entry.   On-line data entry and control functions are provided in the application. Score as follows:

0   All transactions are processed in batch mode.

1   1% to 7% of transactions are interactive data entry.

2   8% to 15% of transactions are interactive data entry.

3   16% to 23% of transactions are interactive data entry.

4   24% to 30% of transactions are interactive data entry.

5   Over 30% of transactions are interactive data entry.

Authors' notes: One of the major problems with the scoring for GSCs is that the guidelines have not been updated in years. Consequently, these scores are not realistic. Nevertheless, industry data has been calculated using these guidelines. Typically, batch receives a score of zero to one; on-line, real-time, telecommunication, or process control systems score a five.

   7. End-user Efficiency.   The on-line functions provided emphasize a design for end-user efficiency. They include the following:

◊ Navigational aids (for example, function keys, jumps, dynamically generated menus)

◊ Menus

◊ On-line help/documentation

◊ Automated cursor movement

◊ Scrolling

◊ Remote printing (via on-line transactions)

◊ Preassigned function keys

◊ Submission of batch jobs from on-line transactions

◊ Cursor selection of screen data

◊ Heavy use of reverse video, highlighting, colors, underlining, and other indicators

◊ Hard copy user documentation of on-line transactions

◊ Mouse interface

◊ Pop-up windows

◊ As few screens as possible to accomplish a business function

◊ Bilingual support (supports two languages; count as four items)

◊ Multilingual support (supports more than two languages; count as six items)

Score as follows:

0   None of the above.

1   One to three of the above.

2   Four to five of the above.

3   Six or more of the above but there are no specific user requirements related to efficiency.

4   Six or more of the above and stated requirements for end-user efficiency are strong enough to require design tasks for human factors to be included (for example, minimize key strokes, maximize defaults, use of templates, etc.).

5   Six or more of the above and stated requirements for end-user efficiency are strong enough to require use of special tools and processes in order to demonstrate that the objectives have been achieved.

Authors' notes: We would expect batch applications with no interactivity to be valued at zero. Most interactive applications have front-end data entry screens, but unless they have templates/defaults built into the application they should be scored at three. If defaults or templates or significant navigational tools are present, score four. In order to score five, there must be user labs to test the useability of the application, rather than the functionality. Real-time, telecommunication, or process control systems may not score anything for this GSC.

    8. On-line Update.   The application provides on-line update for the Internal Logical Files. Score as follows:

0   None.

1   On-line update of one to three control files. Volume of updating is low, and recovery is easy.

2 On-line update of four or more control files. Volume of updating is low, and recovery is easy.

3 On-line update of major internal logical files.

4 In addition, protection against data loss is essential and has been specially designed and programmed in the system.

5 In addition, high volumes bring cost considerations into the recovery process. Highly automated recovery procedures with minimum of operator intervention.

Authors' notes: We would expect batch applications with no interactive update of internal logical files to be valued at zero to two. Most on-line applications update internal logical files and should be scored at three or higher. If protection of data loss has been programmed into the system (not just through back-ups), score four. In order to score five, there must be a highly automated recovery capability built within the application. Real-time, telecommunication, or process control systems often receive a score of four or five.

9. Complex Processing. Complex processing is a characteristic of the application. The categories include the following:

- Sensitive control (for example, special audit processing) and/or application specific security processing
- Extensive logical processing
- Extensive mathematical processing
- Much exception processing resulting in incomplete transactions that must be processed again; for example, incomplete ATM transactions caused by TP interruption, missing data values, or failed edits.
- Complex processing to handle multiple input/output possibilities; for example, multi-media, device independence.

Score this characteristic as follows:

0 None of the above.

1 Any one of the above.

2 Any two of the above.

3 Any three of the above.

4 Any four of the above.

5 All five of the above.

Authors' notes: With the prior GSCs, each individual guideline provided a little more than the previous score. This GSC credits five separate and individual characteristics. First, does the application provide security such that certain individuals see or enter data that others cannot? Second, is there a significant amount of logical (if, then, else) processing? Third, is there extensive mathematical (more than addition/subtraction/simple math) processing? Fourth, is there complex editing or validation? Fifth, are there multiple media included in the application?

10. Reusability. The application and the code in the application have been specifically designed, developed, and supported to be usable in other applications. Score as follows:

0   There is no reusable code.

1   Reusable code is used within the application.

2   Less than 10% of the application considered more than one user's needs.

3   Ten percent or more of the application considered more than one user's needs.

4   The application was specifically packaged and/or documented to ease reuse, and application is customized to user at source code level.

5   The application was specifically packaged and/or documented to ease reuse, and application is customized to use at source code level by means of user parameter maintenance.

Authors' notes: Function Point counting gives credit here with a score of one to those who reuse code. Standardized reusable software provides increased user/owner functionality through increased reliability and consistency. Scores of two through five are assigned based on the resulting functionality and due to the extra effort dedicated to the development, documentation, and testing of code expected to be utilized in other applications.

11. Installation Ease. Conversion and installation ease are characteristics of the application. A conversion and installation plan and/or conversion tools were provided and tested during the system test phase. Score as follows:

0   No special considerations were stated by user, and no special set-up is required for installation.

1   No special considerations were stated by user, but special set-up is required for installation.

2   Conversion and installation requirements were stated by the user, and conversion and installation guides were provided and tested. The impact of conversion on the project is not considered to be important.

3   Conversion and installation requirements were stated by the user, and conversion and installation guides were provided and tested. The impact of conversion on the project is considered to be important.

4   In addition to (2), automated conversion and installation tools were provided and tested.

5   In addition to (3), automated conversion and installation tools were provided and tested.

Authors' notes: Developers are often required to devote significant effort to the conversion of pre-existing data into new data files or to populate the files with actual data or to develop installation software, such as porting. Functional advantages occur to the users through improved schedules and increased consistency. Consider the difficulty or ease of conversion and installation requirements, and assign the score in relationship to their significance.

12. Operational Ease.   Operational ease is characteristic of the application. Effective start-up, back-up, and recovery procedures were provided and tested during the system test phase. The application minimizes the need for manual activities, such as tape mounts, paper handling, and direct on-location manual intervention. Score as follows:

0   No special operational consideration other than the normal back-up procedures were stated by the user.

1-4   Select the following items that apply to the application. Each item has a point value of one, except as noted otherwise:
- Effective start-up, back-up, and recovery processes were provided but operator intervention is required.
- Effective start-up, back-up, and recovery processes were provided but no operator intervention is required (count as two items).
- The application minimizes the need for tape mounts.
- The application minimizes the need for paper handling.

5   Application is designed for unattended operation. Unattended operation means *no operator intervention* is required to operate the system other than to start up or shut down the application. Automatic error recovery is a feature of the application.

Authors' notes: Unless we are counting a legacy system, we should score one each for the lack of tape mounts and the lack of paper (punched cards, punched paper tapes). We should count three if operator intervention is required for start-up, back-up, and recovery. Four would be assigned if no operator intervention is required. Five is assigned to an application that runs and recovers automatically from errors on its own—a lights-out operation.

13. Multiple Sites.   The application has been specifically designed, developed, and supported to be installed at multiple sites for multiple organizations. Score as follows:

0   There is no user requirement to consider the needs of more than one user/installation site.

1   Needs of multiple sites were considered in the design, and the application is designed to operate only under identical hardware and software environments.

2   Needs of multiple sites were considered in the design, and the application is designed to operate only under similar hardware and/or software environments.

3   Needs of multiple sites were considered in the design, and the application is designed to operate under different hardware and/or software environments.

4   Documentation and support plan are provided and tested to support the application at multiple sites, and application is as described by (1) or (2).

5   Documentation and support plan are provided and tested to support the application at multiple sites, and application is as described by (3).

Authors' notes: We consider within this characteristic the increased user functionality and the effort required to deliver an application which will include software and/or hardware installable at multiple sites; this could reflect just the input devices, such as terminals or PCs. Is the software/hardware identical, similar, or different? Are documentation support plans to be provided and tested?

14. Facilitate Change.   The application has been specifically designed, developed, and supported to facilitate change. Examples include the following:

- Flexible query/report capability is provided.
- Business control data is grouped in tables maintainable by the user.

Score as follows:

0   There is no special user requirement to design the application to minimize or facilitate change.

1-5   Select which of the following items apply to the application:

- Flexible query/report facility is provided that can handle simple requests; for example, *and/or* logic applied to only one internal logical file (count as one item).

- Flexible query/report facility is provided that can handle requests of average complexity; for example *and/or* logic applied to more than one internal logical file (count as two items).

- Flexible query/report facility is provided that can handle complex requests; for example, *and/or* logic combinations on one or more internal logical files (count as three items).

- Control data is kept in tables that are maintained by the user with on-line interactive processes, but changes take effect only on the next business day.
- Control data is kept in tables that are maintained by the user with on-line interactive processes, and the changes take effect immediately (count as two items).

Authors' notes: We address two separate categories in this GSC, much the same as GSC 9 had five separate categories. The first area deals with query/report writer capability often provided by languages such as SQL or Focus; scores of zero to three are assigned to this particular characteristic, which is becoming more popular to computer literate users. The second area and the last two questions relate to the interactivity in which data and/or control is maintained within/by the application. Interactive, real time, telecommunication, or process control systems would typically be counted with the last two points.

VALUE ADJUSTMENT FACTOR (VAF)

The fourteen General System Characteristics (GSCs) are summarized into the Value Adjustment Factor (VAF). When applied, the VAF adjusts the Unadjusted Function Point count +/-35 % to produce the final Adjusted Function Point Count.

As a general rule, we would expect a simple batch application to have a total score (Total Degree of Influence, TDI) less than 15, a front end batch application to be between 15 and 30, an interactive application to be between 30 and 45, and a real-time, telecommunication, or process control system to be between 30 and 60. The following steps provide the procedure to calculate the Value Adjustment Factor (VAF):

1. Evaluate the fourteen General System Characteristics (GSCs) on a scale from zero to five to determine the Degree of Influence (DI) for each of the GSC descriptions.
2. Add the Degrees of Influence (DIs) for all fourteen General System Characteristics (GSCs) to produce the Total Degree of Influence (TDI).
3. Use the application's TDI in the following equation to produce the Value Adjustment Factor (VAF):

$$VAF = (TDI * 0.01) + 0.65$$

7

CALCULATING AND APPLYING FUNCTION POINTS

INTRODUCTION

This chapter will use the catalog business previously exampled. Chapter 6 described the definitions, rules, and guidelines for identifying the Value Adjustment Factor which is calculated based on the identification of the fourteen General System Characteristics (GSCs). This chapter will utilize the results of the identification of data and transactional function types as well as the values obtained from identifying the GSCs to calculate a Final Function Point count. Detailed guidance is contained within the IFPUG *Counting Practices Manual.*

FINAL ADJUSTED FUNCTION POINT COUNT

The total process used to size function points was presented in previous chapters and is repeated here. The counting process can be summarized by the following seven steps:

1. Determine the type of Function Point count
2. Identify the application boundary
3. Identify all data functions and their complexity
4. Identify all transactional functions and their complexity
5. Determine the Unadjusted Function Point count†
6. Determine the Value Adjustment Factor—fourteen General System Characteristics*
7. Calculate the final Adjusted Function Point Count*

Remember that the application boundary separates the application being measured from the user domain and/or other independent applications. The data functions relate to the logical data stored and available for update and retrieval. The transactional functions, external inputs (EIs), external outputs (EOs), and external inquiries (EQs), perform the processes of updates, retrieval, outputs, etc. (transactions you would expect to see in a process model). Each has its own unadjusted function point weight based on its unique complexity matrix. The General System Characteristics (GSCs) are each evaluated independently and assigned a unique value between zero (0) and five (5). These scores are summed to calculate a Total Degree of Influence. Then, the Total Degree of Influence is used in a separate calculation to determine the Value Adjustment Factor (VAF). Finally, the total value of the Unadjusted Function Points is multiplied by the VAF in order to obtain a Final Adjusted Function Point Count.

Recall the catalog example. The file folder of descriptions for each item is counted as an internal logical file (ILF). If we determine that the only key (and record element type, RET) is the item number and that there are thirty separate and distinct fields, we count one low ILF. When we add items to that file folder, assuming that there are more than fifteen fields or data element types (DETs) but only one file type referenced (FTR) which would be the descriptions file, we count one average external input (EI).

When we change descriptions, assuming again that there are more than fifteen DETs but one FTR, we count another average EI. When we delete items from the folder when they are no longer available, we have less than five DETs (fields counted which cross the boundary into the application; see the rules for EIs if this is confusing) and the same FTR. Consequently, we have a low complexity EI. When we retrieve the description from the file, we display more than nineteen DETs from one file (FTR) and count the transaction as an average External Inquiry (EQ).

We said there were two other file folders updated within the application which contained inventory data and sales data. Let's assume that the data and transactional function types are weighted the same as the description file and its transactions. We would count two more low complexity ILFs, four more average complexity EIs, two more low EIs, and two more average complexity EQs.

*Discussed in this chapter

The report at the end of the month that totals our sales for the month is counted as an External Output (EO). If that report contains more than nineteen DETs and retrieves data from two or more FTRs, we count a high complexity EO.

The file maintained within another application, which contains vendor addresses, is used when we produce that report and consequently was counted as an FTR for the EO, but it is also counted as an external interface file (EIF). Let's make the assumption that it is a low complexity EIF.

We can assign these appropriate point values based upon their complexity (the functions and their respective values will be displayed later within a table):

3 low EIs are valued at 3 points each for a total of 9.

6 average EIs are valued at 4 points each for a total of 24.

1 high EO is valued at 7 points for a total of 7.

3 average EQs are valued at 4 points each for a total of 12.

3 low ILFs are valued at 7 points each for a total of 21.

1 low EIF is valued at 5 points for a total of 5.

The total Unadjusted Function Point Count would be 78.

Refer to the previous chapter, and attempt to assign Degrees of Influence (DIs), to the General System Characteristics (GSCs). The editors have selected the following values from their view of this example:

1.	Data communications	4
2.	Distributed data processing	0
3.	Performance	3
4.	Heavily used configuration	2
5.	Transaction rate	3
6.	On-line data entry	5
7.	End user efficiency	4
8.	On-line update	3
9.	Complex processing	1
10.	Reuseability	0
11.	Installation ease	0
12.	Operational ease	3
13.	Multiple sites	1
14.	Facilitate change	2
Total Degree of Influence (TDI)		31

Using the formula:

Value Adjustment Factor (VAF) = (TDI * 0.01) + 0.65,

the VAF in this example is equal to .96 or 96/100
    The Application Function Point Count or the Project Function Point Count for
this first install, with no conversion functionality, is equal to

(the Unadjusted Function Point Count) * (the VAF)

or for this example

(78 Unadjusted Function Points) (.96 (96/100))

for a Final Adjusted Function Point Count of 74.88, which we would round to 75.

To collect and record this information we would actually use a Function Point
Count Summary and a Function Point Calculation Table or worksheet like those of
Tables 7.1 and 7.2.

DEVELOPMENT PROJECT FUNCTION POINT COUNT

A Development Project Function Point Count consists of three components of functionality:

- ↪ Application Unadjusted Function Point Count consisting of the EIs, EOs,
  EQs, ILFs, and EIFs
- ↪ Conversion functionality to transfer previous data into the new ILFs through
  software (this often consists of the input of the old data files [counted as EIs
  or input data into the already counted new ILFs] and possibly an EO for a
  conversion report)
- ↪ The Application Value Adjustment Factor

The count above could be considered a Development Project Function Point Count
or an Application Function Point Count, discussed later. These counts will also be
included in our case studies.

Development Project Function Point (DFP) Calculation

The following formula is used to calculate the Development Project Function Point
Count:

TABLE 7.1 Function Point Count Summary

FUNCTION POINT COUNT SUMMARY

Project Number

Date of Count

Project Name

Counters Name

Instructions: Enter all function types included. For development and initial Function Point counts there will not be any entries in the Before columns. Annotate all function types added by the conversion. You may wish to use different sheets for files and transactions.

DESCRIPTION	TYPE ILF/EIF EI/EO/EQ	DETs After	DETs Before	RETs/FTRs After	RETs/FTRs Before	COMPLEXITY After	COMPLEXITY Before
File Folder	ILF	30		1		L	
Descriptions–Add	EI	>15		1		A	
Descriptions–Change	EI	>15		1		A	
Descriptions–Delete	EI	< 5		1		L	
Descriptions–Retrieve	EQ	>19		1		A	
Inventory	ILF	30		1		L	
Inventory–Add	EI	>15		1		A	
Inventory–Change	EI	>15		1		A	
Inventory–Delete	EI	< 5		1		L	
Inventory–Retrieve	EQ	>19		1		A	
Sales	ILF	30		1		L	
Sales–Add	EI	>15		1		A	
Sales–Change	EI	>15		1		A	
Sales–Delete	EI	< 5		1		L	
Sales–Retrieve	EQ	>19		1		A	
End of Month Report	EO	>19		>2		H	
Vendor Address File	EIF					L	

95

TABLE 7.2 Function Point Calculation Table

Project Number   **Project Name**

Type of Count: Development Project / Application Count (circle one)

Phase of Count: Proposal / Requirements / Design / Code / Test / Delivery (circle)

Date of Count   **Counter's Name**

* Function Types	Low	Average	High	Total
External Inputs	3×3	6×4	$\times 6$	33
External Outputs	$\times 4$	$\times 5$	1×7	7
External Inquiries	$\times 3$	3×4	$\times 6$	12
Internal Logical Files	3×7	$\times 10$	$\times 15$	21
External Interface Files	1×5	$\times 7$	$\times 10$	5

Total Unadjusted Function Points (UFPs) = 78

GENERAL SYSTEMS CHARACTERISTICS

Characteristic	Degree of Influence	Characteristic	Degree of Influence
1. Data Communication	4	8. On-line Update	3
2. Distributed Functions	0	9. Complex Processing	1
3. Performance	3	10. Reuseability	0
4. Heavily Used Configuration	2	11. Installation Ease	0
5. Transaction Rate	3	12. Operational Ease	3
6. On-line Data Entry	5	13. Multiple Site	1
7. End-User Efficiency	4	14. Facilitate Change	2
		Total Degree of Influence =	31
		Value Adjustment Factor (VAF) = .65 + (.01 × TDI) =	.96
		Final Function Point Count (FP) = UFP × VAF =	75

*Development Function Point Count includes function types added by the conversion.

Application Function Point Count does not include conversion requirements.

An application count after an enhancement must include all existing function types, including those unchanged.

If information on all existing function types is not available, the application adjusted function point count can be computed using the formula DFP = (UFP + CFP)*VAF.

$$DFP = (UFP + CFP) * VAF$$

Where

DFP = Development Project Function Point Count
UFP = Unadjusted Function Point Count
CFP = Function Points included by a conversion of data
VAF = Value Adjustment Factor

ENHANCEMENT PROJECT FUNCTION POINT COUNT

An Enhancement Project Function Point Count also consists of three, but somewhat different, components of functionality:

- Application Unadjusted Function Point Count consisting of the EIs, EOs, EQs, ILFs, and EIFs which are
  - Added by the enhancement project (functions which did not previously exist; for example, a new EQ or three new EIs, a new ILF, a new EQ, and a new EO)
  - Changed by the enhancement project (functions that previously existed but now have different fields or require different processing)
  - Deleted by the enhancement project (functions that have been deleted from the application; for example, a deleted report)
- Conversion functionality to transfer previous data into the new ILFs through software (this often consists of the input of the old data files and possibly an EO for a conversion report)
- Two Application Value Adjustment Factors (there could be a change of VAFs as a part of the project; in which case, there would be a prior VAF and a new VAF)

We have provided an example of an enhancement in our case studies. Remember that an enhancement project most likely will result in a change to the installed or Application Function Point Count. The change will not be additive to the previous Application Function Point Count.

Enhancement Project Function Point (EFP) Calculation

The following formula is used to calculate the Enhancement Project Function Point Count:

$$EFP = [(ADD + CHGA + CFP) * VAFA] + (DEL * VAFB)$$

Where

EFP = Enhancement Project Function Point Count

ADD = Unadjusted Function Point Count of those functions added by the enhancement project

CHGA = Unadjusted Function Point Count of those functions modified by the enhancement project (this reflects the value of the functions after the modifications have occurred, not just the fields added by the modification; a typical error is to count only DETs and FTRs/RETs changed, but everything about that function should be counted to consider effort involved with the testing of existing functionality as well as that changed)

CFP = Function Points included by a conversion of data

VAFA = Value Adjustment Factor of the application *after* the enhancement project

DEL = Unadjusted Function Point Count of those functions that were deleted by the enhancement project

VAFB = Value Adjustment Factor of the application *before* the enhancement project

APPLICATION FUNCTION POINT COUNT

An Application Function Point Count consists of two components of functionality (conversion functionality is not included, unless we are counting an application on its own which performs conversions):

↬ Application Unadjusted Function Point Count consisting of the EIs, EOs, EQs, ILFs, and EIFs
↬ The Application Value Adjustment Factor

There are two different times when we should perform an Application Function Point Count:

↬ When the application is initially delivered
↬ When an enhancement project has changed the value of the application's functionality

When the enhancement project is installed, the previous Application Function Point Count must be updated to recognize modifications to the application. The functionality for the application could have been changed by

↪ Adding (new) functionality, increasing the Function Point size of the application

↪ Changing functionality by increasing, decreasing, or having no effect on the Function Point size of the application

↪ Deleting functionality, decreasing the Function Point size of the application

↪ Making changes to the Value Adjustment Factor adding, decreasing, or having no effect on the Function Point size of the application

There are two different counting formulas to reflect these variations. The Initial Application Function Point (AFP) is calculated by the equation

$$AFP = ADD * VAF$$

where

AFP = initial Application Function Point Count

ADD = Unadjusted Function Point Count of those functions installed by the development project

VAF = Value Adjustment Factor

The application Function Point (AFP) after an enhancement is calculated with the equation

$$AFP = [(UFPB + ADD + CHGA) - (CHGB + DEL)] * VAFA$$

Where

AFP   = Application Adjusted Function Point Count

UFPB   = Application Unadjusted Function Point Count *before* the enhancement project

ADD   = Unadjusted Function Point Count of those functions added by the enhancement project

CHGA = Unadjusted Function Point Count of those functions changed by the enhancement project (this reflects the function point value *after* the change)

CHGB = Unadjusted Function Point Count of those functions changed by the enhancement *before* the change (this reflects the function point value *before* the enhancement project)

DEL   = Unadjusted Function Point Count of those functions deleted by the enhancement project

VAFA = Value Adjustment Factor of the application *after* the enhancement project

Function Point Counting worksheets are provided in the Appendix to assist you in counting.

CHAPTER

8

BASIC FUNCTION POINT COUNTING EXERCISES

INTRODUCTION

The following two case studies are intended to be used as instructional guides to further your understanding of how the Function Point Counting method is applied. The two case studies presented include new development and enhancement. As part of the enhancement count study, an application count is also computed. Chapter 9 will describe in detail the counting guidelines for counting in a Graphical User Interface environment. The first two studies make use of primitive functional diagrams. A generic diagramming technique was used to illustrate that there are no implied links between specific system diagramming techniques and the Function Point methodology. The two cases are laid out in a step-by-step review of the counting method. Remember, to conduct a Function Point analysis, you must perform the following:

1. Determine the type of Function Point count
2. Identify the application boundary
3. Identify all data functions and their complexity

4. Identify all transactional functions and their complexity
5. Determine the Unadjusted Function Point Count
6. Determine the Value Adjustment Factor—fourteen General System Characteristics
7. Calculate the final Adjusted Function Point Count

CASE STUDY I—NEW DEVELOPMENT CASE STUDY

Our first case study will be a new development project. Since there are no conversion requirements, the development project Function Point count will be the same as the application Function Point count. Presented first is a detailed requirements document followed by a primitive system flow and then a walkthrough of the count and calculation.

Requirements Document

The David Consulting Group plans to automate their accounts payable system. It will interface with existing banking, help, and purchase order (PO) systems (systems, not files). Determine the Development Function Point count based on the processing requirements indicated in the following paragraphs for the accounts payable system. This will be a menu driven system. In order to enter the accounts payable system, the user must make selections from a main menu. The menu(s) will have the following options:

1. Invoices
   a. Add an invoice
   b. Display an invoice
   c. Change an invoice
   d. Cancel an invoice
2. Payments
   a. Retrieve payments due
   b. Generate payments
3. Vendors
   a. Add a vendor
   b. Display vendor information
   c. Change vendor information

Invoices

1. Invoice data will be maintained in an Invoice File utilizing the PO number as the primary key to the file.
   a. Invoices will be entered upon receipt with the following data:

⇨ PO number
⇨ vendor name
⇨ vendor billing address (3 lines permitted for street/post office box)
⇨ vendor billing address city
⇨ vendor billing address state
⇨ vendor billing address zip
⇨ date of invoice
⇨ date invoice received
⇨ product/service
⇨ terms
⇨ payment due date
⇨ amount billed

A function key will initiate the edit and save the above data. The PO number, vendor name, and the amount billed will be validated against the PO file (an externally maintained file within the PO system); the vendor name and address will be validated against the vendor file (internally maintained). Error messages will be returned.

There will be drop down list boxes to display:
⇨ outstanding purchase orders by PO number, vendor name, and amount billed from the PO file.
⇨ vendor name and mailing address as above (street, city, state, and zip) from the vendor file.

b. Invoices may be displayed with the same data as contained in list above in paragraph 1a. Selection will be by PO number and a function key. A message will be returned if the PO does not exist in the invoice file. The identical drop down list box will be available to assist in the selection.

c. All fields contained in paragraph 1a may be changed except the PO number, which is the key required to access and change the proper record in the invoice file. The same editing and list boxes discussed in paragraph 1a will be available. A function key will initiate the edit and save the data.

d. An invoice may be deleted by selecting the PO number and a function key. A message will be returned if the PO does not exist in the invoice file.

2. Payment information will be entered in a second record within the invoice file using the PO number and a payment date as the secondary key. The invoice file will contain all of the fields from paragraphs 1a and 2.

a. The user will select payments due between two selected dates and will be able to scroll through invoices with payment due. The user will enter the two dates and a function key. Invoices with payments due between the selected dates will be displayed with the following data:
⇨ PO number
⇨ vendor name

    ⇜ date of invoice

    ⇜ date invoice received

    ⇜ payment due date

    ⇜ terms

    ⇜ amount billed

    ⇜ previous payment dates

    ⇜ amounts paid on those dates

    ⇜ current balance due

    The amounts previously paid by date will be discussed in paragraph 2b. The user may also request that this retrieval be printed.

  b. Payments can be generated by selecting the PO number (must be in the invoice file) and entering the payment date (must be a future date), the amount to be paid, and a function key. Error messages are returned. The payment dates, amounts paid, and current balance due will be saved to the invoice file. The payment required will be passed by file to the banking system at the close of each business day. This file will contain the payment date, payment amount, PO number, vendor name, and vendor billing street address, city, state, and zip. All information will be retrieved from the invoice file and validated against the vendor file to ensure a correct address.

3. Vendor information will be maintained in a vendor file using a vendor name as the primary key to the file.

  a. A new vendor may be added with the following data:

    ⇜ vendor name

    ⇜ vendor billing address (3 lines)

    ⇜ city

    ⇜ state

    ⇜ zip

    ⇜ vendor point of contact

    ⇜ vendor phone number

    ⇜ function key.

    The vendor name distinguishes between vendors with more than one location. Errors are returned. The identical vendor drop down list, discussed in paragraph 1a, will be provided.

  b. Vendor data may be displayed with the same information as contained in paragraph 3a. Selection will be by vendor and a function key. A message will be returned if the vendor does not exist in the vendor file. The vendor drop down list will be provided.

  c. All fields contained in paragraph 3a may be changed except the vendor name, which is the key required to access and change the proper record in the vendor file. The same editing and list box provided in paragraph 3a will be available. A function key will initiate the edit and save the data. There is no plan to delete vendor information.

4. Two levels of help (window and field) will be available from two externally maintained help files. There will be one set of help text, for each selection, which may be scrollable.

5. Other characteristics of the invoice system will be as follows:

    ↪ Application is more than a front end but supports only one type of TP communications protocol

    ↪ Will not be distributed processing

    ↪ No special performance requirements

    ↪ No explicit or implicit operational restrictions

    ↪ No peak transaction period

    ↪ In addition to other features of this on-line system already discussed, there will be automated cursor movement and cursor selection of screen data; there are no specific user requirements related to efficiency

    ↪ On-line update of ILFs but no protection against data loss

    ↪ No complex processing

    ↪ Most (more than 50%) of the application and code should be designed, developed, and supported to be usable in other applications

    ↪ No special conversion, installation, or set-up requirements

    ↪ The application will minimize the need for both tape mounts and paper handling; effective start-up, back-up, and recovery process, but operator intervention is required

    ↪ Needs of multiple sites must be considered in the design; application will operate under similar hardware and software environments

    ↪ No flexible query/report capability; control data will be maintained inter-actively and take effect immediately.

Exercises in Counting

Step-by-step, we will now begin the process of sizing the discussed requirements document using the Function Point counting rules described in Chapters 3 through 8.

Determine the Type of Function Point Count.   From reading the requirements document we know that this is a new development effort without a conversion effort.

Identify the Application Boundary.   After reading the specifications we are able to draft a primitive functional flow of the system as shown in Figure 8.1.

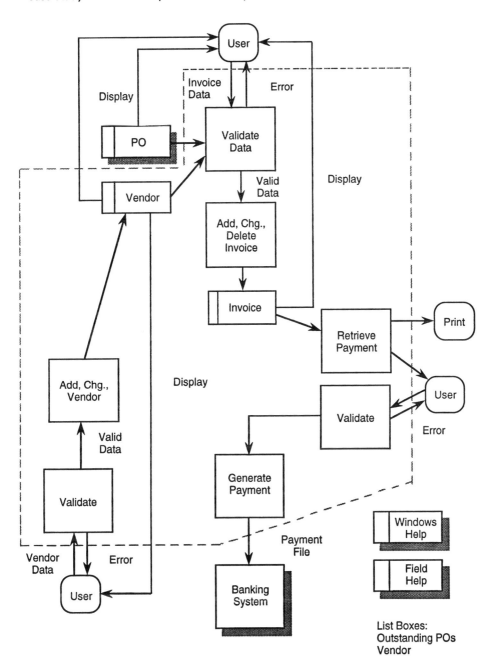

FIGURE 8.1   Functional Flow of Accounts Payable System

Identify All Data Functions and Their Complexity. Reading the requirements we can identify two ILFs in this system:

1. Invoice File—ILF
   - ✑ Invoice data will be maintained in an Invoice File utilizing the PO number as the primary key to the file.
   - ✑ Payment information will be entered in a second record within the invoice file using the PO number and a payment date as the secondary key. The invoice file will contain all of the fields from paragraphs 1a and 2.

   The resulting count for this ILF would be 15 DETs and 2 RETs (PO Number and payment date). If we look at the matrices for applying the weights we see that a value of Low, or 7 Function Points, applies.

2. Vendor File—ILF
   - ✑ Vendor information will be maintained in a vendor file using a vendor name as the primary key to the file. A new vendor may be added with the following data: vendor name, vendor billing address (3 lines), city, state, zip, vendor point of contact, vendor phone number.

   The resulting count for this ILF would be 7 DETs and 1 RET. If we look at the matrices for applying the weights we see that a value of Low, or 7 Function Points, applies.

Reading the requirements we can also identify three EIFs:

1. PO File—EIF
   - ✑ The PO number, vendor name, and the amount billed will be validated against the PO file (an externally maintained file within the PO system).

   The resulting count for this EIF would be 3 DETs and 1 RET. If we look at the matrices for applying the weights we see that a value of Low, or 5 Function Points, applies.

2. Windows Help File—EIF
3. Field Help File—EIF
   - ✑ Two levels of help (window and field) will be available from two externally maintained help files.

   These files contain less than 20 DETs and only one RET; therefore, the resulting value would be Low, or 5 Function Points each.

Our unadjusted count for Data Function Types is shown in Table 8.1.

TABLE 8.1 Count of Data Function Types

Function Types	Low	Average	High	Total
Internal Logical Files	2 × 7	× 10	× 15	14
External Interface Files	3 × 5	× 7	× 10	15

Identify All Transactional Functions And Their Complexity. Reading the requirements we can identify six external inputs in this system:

1. Add Invoice—EI
   - ↬ Invoices will be entered upon receipt with the following data: PO number, vendor name, vendor billing address (3 lines permitted for street/post office box), vendor billing address city, vendor billing address state, vendor billing address zip, date of invoice, date invoice received, product/service, terms, payment due date, and amount billed. A function key will initiate the edit and save the above data. Error messages will be returned.

   The resulting count for this EI would be 14 DETs (including 1 DET each for error messages and the command keys) and 3 FTRs (Invoice, PO, Vendor). If we look at the matrices for applying the weights we see that a value of High, or 6 Function Points, applies. Note: Each of our EIs will add a total of one DET for error/confirmation messages and a total of one DET for command key(s).

2. Change Invoice—EI
   - ↬ All fields contained in paragraph 1a may be changed except the PO number, which is the key required to access and change the proper record in the invoice file. The same editing and list boxes provided in paragraph 1a will be available. A function key will initiate the edit and save the data.

   The resulting count for this EI would be 14 DETs and 3 FTRs (Invoice, PO, Vendor). If we look at the matrices for applying the weights we see that a value of High, or 6 Function Points, applies.

3. Delete Invoice—EI
   - ↬ An invoice may be deleted by selecting the PO number and a function key. A message will be returned if the PO does not exist in the invoice file.

   The resulting count for this EI would be 3 DETs (PO number, error messages, and command key) and 1 FTR. If we look at the matrices for applying the weights we see that a value of Low, or 3 Function Points, applies.

4. Generate Payments—EI
   - ↬ Payments can be generated by selecting the PO number (must be in the invoice file) and entering the payment date, the amount to be paid, and a function key. Error messages are returned.

   The resulting count for this EI would be 5 DETs and 1 FTRs. If we look at the matrices for applying the weights we see that a value of Low, or 3 Function Points, applies.

5. Add Vendor—EI
   - ↬ A new vendor may be added with the following data: vendor name, vendor billing address (3 lines), city, state, and zip, vendor point of contact,

vendor phone number, and a function key. The vendor name distinguishes between vendors with more than one location. Errors are returned.

The resulting count for this EI would be 9 DETs and 1 FTRs. If we look at the matrices for applying the weights we see that a value of Low, or 3 Function Points, applies.

6. Change Vendor—EI

   ↝ All fields contained in paragraph 3a may be changed except the vendor name, which is the key required to access and change the proper record in the vendor file. The same editing and list box provided in paragraph 3a will be available. A function key will initiate the edit and save the data.

   ↝ The resulting count for this EI would be 9 DETs and 1 FTRs. If we look at the matrices for applying the weights we see that a value of Low, or 3 Function Points, applies (Table 8.2).

TABLE 8.2   Count of External Inputs

Function Types	Low	Average	High	Total
External Inputs	4 × 3	× 4	2 × 6	24

Reading the requirements we can also identify eight external inquiries:

1. Outstanding POs List Box—EQ
2. Vendor List Box—EQ

   ↝ There will be drop down list boxes to display outstanding purchase orders by PO number, vendor name, amount billed from the PO file, vendor name, and mailing address (street, city, state, and zip) from the vendor file.

   The resulting count (output side) for the outstanding PO and Vendor List Boxes EQs would be 3 DETs and 1 FTR, and 5 DETs and 1 FTR respectively. If we look at the matrices for applying the weights we see that values of Low, or 3 Function Points each, would apply.

3. Display an Invoice—EQ

   ↝ Invoices may be displayed with the same data as contained in add/change functions: PO number, vendor name, vendor billing address (3 lines permitted for street/post office box), vendor billing address city, vendor billing address state, vendor billing address zip, date of invoice, date invoice received, product/service, terms, payment due date, and amount billed.

   The resulting count (output side) for this EQ would be 12 DETs and 1 FTR. If we look at the matrices for applying the weights we see that a value of Low, or 3 Function Points, would apply.

4. Retrieve Payment Screen—EQ

5. Retrieve Payment Print—EQ

   ↪ Invoices with payments due between the selected dates will be displayed with the following data: PO number, vendor name, date of invoice, date invoice received, payment due date, terms, amount billed, previous payment dates, amounts paid on those dates, and current balance due. The user may also request that this retrieval be printed.

The resulting count (output side) for these two EQs (on-line and printed) would be 10 DETs and 1 FTR for each. If we look at the matrices for applying the weights we see that a value of Low, or 3 Function Points, would apply to each.

6. DisplayVendor Information—EQ

   ↪ Vendor data may be displayed with the same information as contained in the change function: vendor name, vendor billing address (3 lines), city, state, zip, vendor point of contact and vendor phone number.

The resulting count (output side) for this EQ would be 7 DETs and 1 FTR. If we look at the matrices for applying the weights we see that a value of Low, or 3 Function Points, would apply.

7. Windows Help—EQ

8. Field Help—EQ

   ↪ Two levels of help (window and field) will be available from two externally maintained help files. There will be one set of help text, for each selection, which may be scrollable.

The resulting count (output side) for these EQs would be less than 20 DETs and 1 FTR. If we look at the matrices for applying the weights we see that a value of Low, or 3 Function Points, would apply for each (Table 8.3).

TABLE 8.3   Count of External Inquiries

Function Types	Low	Average	High	Total
External Inquiries	8 × 3	× 4	× 6	24

Reading the requirements we can identify one External Output in this system:

1. File To Bank System—EO

   ↪ The payment required will be passed by file to the banking system at the close of each business day. This file will contain the payment date, payment amount, PO number, vendor name, vendor billing street address, city, state, zip. All information will be retrieved from the invoice file and validated against the vendor file to ensure a correct address.

The resulting count for this EO would be less than 8 DETs and 2 FTRs. If we look at the matrices for applying the weights we see that a value of Average, or 5 Function Points, would apply (Table 8.4).

TABLE 8.4   Count of External Output

Function Types	Low	Average	High	Total
External Output	×4	1×5	×7	5

Determine the Unadjusted Function Point Count.   The Unadjusted Function Point count is computed from the sum of all the data and transaction function Types and is displayed in Table 8.5.

TABLE 8.5   Unadjusted Function Point Count for the Accounts Payable System

Function Types	Low	Average	High	Total
External Inputs	4×3	×4	2×6	24
External Outputs	×4	1×5	×7	5
External Inquiries	8×3	×4	×6	24
Internal Logical Files	2×7	×10	×15	14
External Interface Files	3×5	×7	×10	15
			Total Unadjusted Function Points (UFPs) =	82

Determine the Value Adjustment Factor—14 General System Characteristics.   The requirements define what characteristics will be present for this system. Other characteristics of the invoice system will be as follows:

- ↩ Application is more than a front end but supports only one type of TP communications protocol
- ↩ Will not be distributed processing
- ↩ No special performance requirements
- ↩ No explicit or implicit operational restrictions
- ↩ No peak transaction period
- ↩ In addition to other features of this on-line system already discussed, there will be automated cursor movement and cursor selection of screen data; there are no specific user requirements related to efficiency
- ↩ On-line update of ILFs but no protection against data loss
- ↩ No complex processing
- ↩ Most (more than 50%) of the application and code should be designed, developed, and supported to be useable in other applications

↝ No special conversion, installation, or set-up requirements

↝ The application will minimize the need for both tape mounts and paper handling; effective start-up, back-up, and recovery process, but operator intervention required

↝ Needs of multiple sites must be considered in the design; application will operate under similar hardware and software environments

↝ No flexible query/report capability; control data will be maintained interactively and take effect immediately

Using this information we can then compute our Total Degree of Influence to be used in the next step of our process (Table 8.6).

TABLE 8.6   General Systems Characteristics for the Accounts Payable System

Characteristic	Degree of Influence	Characteristic	Degree of Influence
1. Data Communications	4	8. Online Update	3
2. Distributed Factors	0	9. Complex Processing	0
3. Performance	0	10. Reusability	3
4. Heavily Used Configuration	0	11. Installation Ease	0
5. Transaction Rate	0	12. Operational Ease	3
6. Online Data Entry	5	13. Multiple Site	2
7. End User Efficiency	3	14. Facilitate Change	2
		Total Degree of Influence = 25	

Calculate the Final Adjusted Function Point Count.   In this step, our final Function Point count is computed using the Value Adjustment Factor and the Unadjusted Function Point count:

$$\text{Value Adjustment Factor (VAF)} = .65 + (.01 \times \text{TDI}) = .90$$
$$\text{Final Function Point Count (FP)} = \text{UFP} \times \text{VAF}$$
$$\text{Final Function Point Count} = .82 \times .90 = 74$$

CASE STUDY 2—ENHANCEMENT CASE STUDY

Our second case study involves the counting of an enhancement project and the resulting (after the enhancement has been completed) application count. There are no conversions associated with this case.

Requirements Document

The previous case study indicated that a newly developed accounts payable system would interface with existing banking, help, and purchase order systems. No changes were required to the help and purchase order systems; however, the new development requirements indicated that the accounts payable system would create and pass a file to the banking system at the close of every business day. This file contains the payment date required, payment amount, PO number, vendor name, and vendor billing street address, city, state, and zip. The banking system must now be enhanced in order to process this incoming file and to generate the appropriate checks. We shall now determine the enhancement Function Point count for the banking system based on the information indicated in the following paragraphs.

1. The Banking system will process the incoming batch file sent by the Accounts Payable system without any edits or validation into two user maintained files: the checking account file and the disbursements file.
   a. The checking account file previously had two record element types and nineteen data element types. This change will require the addition of the PO number to the checking account file. All other fields were previously included.
   b. The disbursements file did not require any changes as a result of this enhancement.
2. The current process to generate checks to pay invoices will be modified. Checks now will be generated with the PO number as a separate memo field by the banking system. Previously, checks contained the following information: preprinted name and address for the David Consulting Group, preprinted check numbers, the payment date, the payment amount, the payee (same as vendor's name), and the payee's street address, city, state, and zip. Previously the checks did not include a memo field. These checks reference only the checking account file when they are created.
3. A printed report will be generated out of the banking file if checks were not produced because of an inadequate balance. The report will appear as shown in Figure 8.2. The last two fields are derived.
4. These transactions will be maintained in a new suspense file until cleared. This file will contain the original payment date, payee, PO number, and payment amount.
   a. There will be a new on-line inquiry to retrieve information from the sus-

Insufficient Funds for Payment Date _____

Payee	PO Number	Payment Amount
-		
-		
-		
-		
-		

Total number of Payees _____   **Total payment amount** _____

FIGURE 8.2   Inadequate Balance Report

pense file. It will display the original payment date, payee, PO number, and payment amount from the suspense file whenever the user enters the payment date and a function key.

b. The suspense file must be updated/cleared by users through an on-line update transaction which will enter a new payment date. This transaction will pass the original payment date, the PO number, the new payment date, and the payment amount to the banking file, disbursement file, and suspense file using a function key. An error message will be returned immediately to the screen if there are insufficient funds to process the request and the transaction cannot be processed.

5. There will be no changes to the banking system's General System Characteristics which are listed as follows:

1. 4	**6.** 5	**11.** 2
2. 0	**7.** 3	**12.** 3
3. 3	**8.** 3	**13.** 3
4. 2	**9.** 3	**14.** 2
5. 3	**10.** 3	

6. Keep in mind that the previous unadjusted Function Point count for the Banking system was 330.

Exercises in Counting

We will now begin the step-by-step process of sizing the above requirements document using the Function Point counting rules described in Chapters 3 through 7.

Determine the Type of Function Point Count.   From reading the requirements document we know that this is an enhancement project without a conversion effort.

Identify the Application Boundary. After reading the specifications we are able to draft a primitive functional flow of the system (Figure 8.3). This allows us to better understand the elements we are working with and identify the functional components.

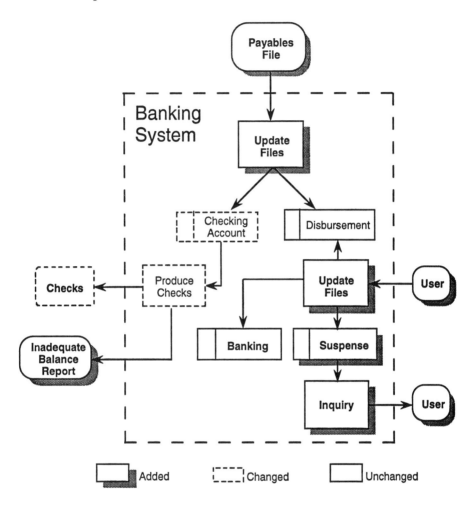

FIGURE 8.3   The Banking System As Modified

Identify All Data Functions and Their Complexity. Reading the requirements we can identify two ILFs in this system (note that the Disbursements File is unchanged and not counted):

1. Checking Account File—ILF
    ↪ The checking account file previously had 2RETs and 19 DETs. This

change will require the addition of the PO number to the checking account file. All other fields were previously included.

The addition of the PO number to the checking account file requires a change to an existing ILF. Based on the counting rules this situation requires the identification of a ILF for an enhancement project. If any changes are made to existing function types, then those function types are counted with the total of DETs and RETs/FTRs which exist after the change.

The resulting count for this changed ILF would be 20 DETs and 2 RETs. If we look at the matrices for applying the weights we see that a value of Average, or 10 Changed Function Points, applies. The previous count of this ILF before the enhancement was 19 DETs and 2 RETs, for a value of Low, or 7 Function Points.

2. Suspense File—ILF

   ↪ These transactions will be maintained in a new suspense file until cleared. This file will contain the original payment date, payee, PO number, and payment amount.

The resulting count for this added ILF would be 4 DETs and 1 RET. If we look at the matrices for applying the weights we see that a value of Low, or 7 Added Function Points, applies.

There are no External Interface Files, EIFs, identified in this enhancement. Our unadjusted count for the Changed Data Function Type is shown in Table 8.7. Our unadjusted count for the Added Data Function Type is shown in Table 8.8.

TABLE 8.7   Count of Changed Data Function Types

Function Types	Low	Average	High	Total
Internal Logical Files	× 7	1 × 10	× 15	10
External Interface Files	× 5	× 7	× 10	0

TABLE 8.8   Count of Added Data Function Types

Function Types	Low	Average	High	Total
Internal Logical Files	1 × 7	× 10	× 15	7
External Interface Files	× 5	× 7	× 10	0

Identify All Transactional Functions and Their Complexity.   Reading the requirements we can identify two External Inputs in this enhancement:

1. Accounts Payable File—EI

   ↪ The banking system will process the new incoming file from the accounts payable system without any edits or validation into two user maintained files, the checking account file and the disbursements file. This file contains the payment date required (this will usually be a future date), payment amount, PO number, vendor name, and vendor billing street address, city, state, and zip. This is an EI, not an ILF or EIF.

The resulting count for this added EI would be 8 DETs and 2 FTRs (Account, Disbursement). If we look at the matrices for applying the weights we see that a value of Average, or 4 Added Function Points, applies.

2. Update/Clear Suspense File—EI
   ↪ The new suspense file must be updated/cleared by users through an on-line update transaction which will enter a new payment date. This transaction will pass the original payment date, the PO number, the new payment date, and the payment amount to the banking file, disbursement file, and suspense file using a function key. An error message will be returned immediately to the screen if there are insufficient funds to process the request and the transaction can not be processed.

The resulting count for this added EI would be 6 DETs and 3 FTRs (Banking, Disbursement, Suspense). If we look at the matrices for applying the weights we see that a value of High, or 6 Added Function Points, applies.

Our unadjusted count for the Added External Inputs is shown in Table 8.9.

TABLE 8.9   Count of Added External Inputs

Function Types	Low	Average	High	Total
External Inputs	× 3	1 × 4	1 × 6	10

Reading the requirements we can identify one external inquiry to be counted in this enhancement:

1. Suspense File—EQ
   ↪ There will be a new on-line inquiry to retrieve information from the suspense file. It will display the original payment date, payee, PO number, and payment amount from the suspense file whenever the user enters the payment date and a function key.

The resulting count (output side) for this added EQ would be 4 DETs and 1 FTR. If we look at the matrices for applying the weights we see that a value of Low, or 3 Added Function Points, applies.

TABLE 8.10   Added Enternal Inquiry

Function Types	Low	Average	High	Total
External Inquiry	1 × 3	× 4	× 6	3

Our unadjusted count for the Added External Inquiry is shown in Table 8.10.

Reading the requirements we can identify two external outputs in this enhancement:

1. Checks—EO

↪ The current process to generate checks to pay invoices will be modified. Checks now will be generated with the PO number as a separate memo field by the banking system. Previously, checks contained the following information: preprinted name and address for the David Consulting Group, preprinted check numbers, the payment date, the payment amount, the payee (same as vendor's name), and the payee's street address, city, state, and zip. They previously did not include a memo field. These checks reference only the checking account file when they are created.

The resulting count for this changed EO would be 8 DETs and 1 FTR. If we look at the matrices for applying the weights we see that a value of Low, or 4 Changed Function Points, applies.

TABLE 8.11   Count of Changed External Output

Function Types	Low	Average	High	Total
External Outputs	1 × 4	× 5	× 7	4

2. Printed Report—EO

↪ A new printed report will be generated out of the banking file if checks were not produced because of an inadequate balance.

The resulting count for this added EO would be 6 DETs and 1 FTR. If we look at the matrices for applying the weights we see that a value of Low, or 4 Added Function Points, applies.

Our unadjusted count for the Changed External Output is shown in Table 8.11. Our unadjusted count for the Added External Output is shown in Table 8.12.

TABLE 8.12   Count of Added External Output

Function Types	Low	Average	High	Total
External Inquiry	1 × 4	× 5	× 7	4

Determine the Unadjusted Function Point Count.   The Unadjusted Function Point count is computed from the added and changed function types as shown in Table 8.13 and Table 8.14

TABLE 8.13   Count of Added Function Types

Function Types	Low	Average	High	Total
External Inputs	×3	1× 4	1× 6	10
External Outputs	1×4	× 5	× 7	4
External Inquiries	1×3	× 4	× 6	3
Internal Logical Files	1×7	×10	×15	7
External Interface Files	×5	× 7	×10	0

Total Added Function Points (UFPs) = 24

TABLE 8.14   Count of Changed Function Types

Function Types	Low	Average	High	Total
External Inputs	×3	×4	×6	0
External Outputs	1×4	×5	×7	4
External Inquiries	×3	×4	×6	0
Internal Logical Files	×7	1×10	×15	10
External Interface Files	×5	×7	×10	0

Total Unadjusted Function Points (UFPs) = 14

Determine the Value Adjustment Factor—Fourteen General System Characteristics.   The General System Characteristics (GSCs) were unchanged. Table 8.15 represents their before and after values.

TABLE 8.15   General Systems Characteristics for the Banking System

Characteristic	Degree of Influence	Characteristic	Degree of Influence
1. Data Communications	4	8. Online Update	3
2. Distributed Factors	0	9. Complex Processing	3
3. Performance	3	10. Reusability	3
4. Heavily Used Configuration	2	11. Installation Ease	2
5. Transaction Rate	3	12. Operational Ease	3
6. Online Data Entry	5	13. Multiple Site	3
7. End User Efficiency	3	14. Facilitate Change	2

Total Degree of Influence = 39

Calculate the Final Adjusted Function Point Count.   In this final step of our Final Function Point count for the enhancement project is computed using the Value Adjustment Factor and the Added and Changed Unadjusted Function Point counts:

Value Adjustment Factor (VAF) = .65 + (.01 × TDI) = 1.04
Enhancement Project Function Points (EFP) = [(ADD + CHGA + CFP) × VAFA]
+ (DEL × VAFB)
Enhancement Project Function Points (EFP) = [(24 + 14 + 0) × 1.04] + (0 × 1.04) =
39.52 or 40

Calculate the Final Adjusted Function Point Count—Application.

The application Function Point count is calculated next, using the following formula

$$AFP = [(UFPB + ADD + CHGA) - (CHGB + DEL)] * VAFA$$

where

AFP   = the application's adjusted Function Point count *after* the enhancement

UFPB = the application's unadjusted Function Point count *before* the enhancement project

ADD   = the unadjusted Function Point count of those functions that were added by the enhancement

CHGA = the unadjusted Function Point count of those functions that were changed by the enhancement project; this number reflects the functions *after* the changes

CHGB = the unadjusted Function Point count of those functions that were changed by the enhancement *before* the changes were made

DEL   = the unadjusted Function Point count of those functions that were deleted by the enhancement

VAFA = the value adjustment factor of the application *after* the enhancement

Using the values we have from the case study we realize the following result:

$$AFP = [(UFPB + ADD + CHGA) - (CHGB + DEL)] × VAFA$$

$$371 = [(330 + 24 + 14) - (11 + 0)] × 1.04$$

9

COUNTING A GRAPHICAL USER INTERFACE (GUI) APPLICATION

INTRODUCTION

Graphical User Interfaces have become very common in the last decade. Although first introduced by Xerox, they became popular in the Apple line of computer, especially the Macintosh. They are now available in many environments such as Windows, Presentation Manager, OPEN LOOK, NeXT, and Motif. GUIs typically include such user functions as listed:

Primary and secondary windows
Icons
Pull-down and pop-up menus and selection lists
Action bars
Dialog boxes
Selection lists permitting point and click capability
Scroll bars
Pushbuttons

Sliders

Spin buttons

Radio buttons

In previous chapters we discussed new development counts, enhancement counts, and application counts. This chapter will describe those same functions using the International Function Point User Group (IFPUG) definitions, rules, and guidelines. Figure 9.1 is a Microsoft GUI screen and is displayed for discussion purposes only.

GUI COUNTING RULES

1. Remember that the application boundary separates the application being measured from the user domain. The data function types relate to the logical data stored and available for update and retrieval. The transactional function types, external inputs (EIs), external outputs (EOs), and external inquiries (EQs), perform the processes of updates, retrieval, outputs, etc. (transactions you

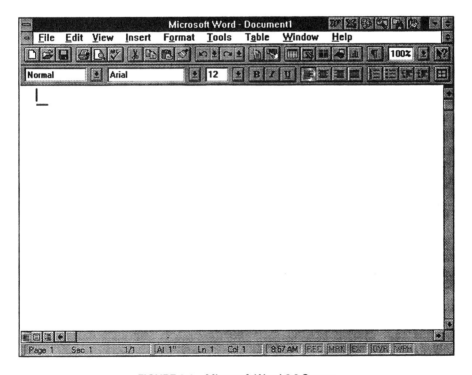

FIGURE 9.1   Microsoft Word 6.0 Screen

would expect to see in a process model). Each has its own Unadjusted Function Point weight based upon its unique complexity matrix.

2. User functions which create, update, or delete data should be counted as external inputs; ensure that the data is being maintained and is not just a screen view. The selection of File Save and File Save As often provide the command key functions for add and change functionality. Don't count the same function twice when multiple keys accomplish the same function.

3. Selection of an item from a pick list is usually a DET on an EI and not a separate EI.

4. User functions that retrieve/extract data based on a user's request/selection and display that data should be counted as external inquiries; this could include a simple list box or typically a File Open without calculated data.

5. User functions that involve the calculation of data in order to display data should be counted as external outputs; this could include File Open.

6. Print functions usually create printed copies of the display and should be counted as additional external inquiries (without calculated data) or external outputs (with calculated data).

7. Print format instructions, however, provide business functionality that should be recognized as an external input (control data).

8. Functions that are automatically provided by Windows or the operating system and not by the application being sized should not be counted; for example, minimize, maximize, etc., unless you are counting Windows itself.

9. Menus, icons, scroll bars, and other navigation devices are not counted unless they return retrieved user data.

10. Exit instructions are also navigational, returning control to the system or calling program, thus are not counted.

11. Individual selections from a menu (action bar, pull-down, pop-up, or iconic) or a pushbutton may serve as the input side of an EQ or the command key to perform an EI or select an EO.

12. Selection lists, spin buttons, or list boxes are counted as EQs when they retrieve and display data; the selection of one of the items displayed by "point and click" or some similar method is not usually a stand-alone function, but a DET.

13. Functions that permit the selection of one choice from a selection of choices available from a slider or radio button count as one DET on the EI or the input side of the EQ and not as one DET for each choice; however, if multiple selections can be accepted, as in check boxes, than each independent selection would count as a DET.

14. Status, informational, and warning messages, other than error or confirmation messages, are usually EOs.

15. Control EIs should be counted for user required functions which ensure compliance with business related functionality.

16. Help is counted normally, with one external inquiry per level of Help per application.

Exercise in Counting a GUI System

We will now begin the step-by-step process of sizing a requirements document using the Function Point counting rules described in Chapters 3 through 7. An independent exercise will be conducted at this point with examples of a GUI system. The approach that we will use to count this existing application is different from the previous two case studies. You are requested to review the screens/windows and identify the function types that should be counted. The screens will be presented first with notes about the capabilities. The Microsoft Windows Calendar application (Figure 9.2) has been selected as our application for sizing. The Calendar application is being displayed for discussion purposes only. This is an existing application that is being counted.

Remember, to conduct a Function Point analysis, you must

1. Determine the type of Function Point count
2. Identify the application boundary
3. Identify all data functions and their complexity

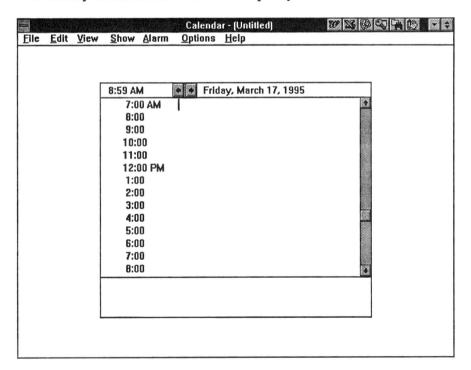

FIGURE 9.2   Microsoft Windows Calendar Application with Action Bar Choices

4. Identify all transactional functions and their complexity
5. Determine the Unadjusted Function Point count
6. Determine the Value Adjustment Factor—fourteen General System Characteristics
7. Calculate the final Adjusted Function Point Count

Determine the Type of Function Point Count. From reading the requirements document we know that this is a new development effort without a conversion effort.

Identify the Application Boundary. After reading the specifications we could draft a primitive functional flow of the system.

Identify all Data Function Types and all Transactional Function Types and their Complexity. We will count the different function types as they are naturally revealed in our functional walkthrough of the application.

Windows Calendar contains a monthly calendar and a daily appointment book. The untitled calendar (primary window) in Figure 9.2 appears after being selected via an icon. The calendar displays the current system time and date.

↪ Clock—EIF

   Information is retrieved from the Windows Clock application. The resulting count for this EIF would be <20 DETs and 1 RET. If we look at the matrices for applying the weights we see that a value of Low, or 5 Function Points, applies.

   We see in Figure 9.3 that the first choice on the action bar is **File.** We find the **New** option and the **Open** option on the pull-down menu under File. **New** returns the untitled calendar. Appointments can be entered next to an appointment time by entering up to eighty characters of text. Notes and reminders (up to three lines) can be entered in the scratch area below. Data may be saved using the **Save As** function. **Open** returns the selected record in the primary window for the current date. Data can be edited and saved using the **Save** function or deleted using the **Edit** function. We can identify and count the following functionality.

↪ Time and Date—EO

   The current time and date is displayed from, and continually updated by, the Windows Clock application. The resulting count for this EO would be 2 DETs and 1 FTR. If we look at the matrices for applying the weights we see that a value of Low, or 4 Function Points, applies.

↪ Open Calendar—EQ

   We can open our calendar for the current date. The currently saved calendar data will be displayed. The resulting count for this EQ would be less than 20

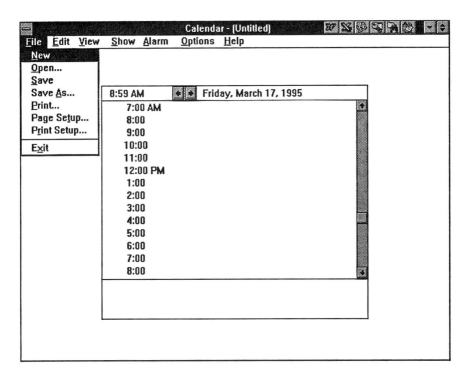

FIGURE 9.3 Microsoft Windows Calendar with File Pull-Down Menu

DETs and 1 FTR on the output side. If we look at the matrices for applying the weights we see that a value of Low, or 3 Function Points, applies.

↪ Enter Calendar Data (**Save As**)—EI
We can enter data for a new calendar date. The resulting count for this EI would be less than 16 DETs and 1 FTR. If we look at the matrices for applying the weights we see that a value of Low, or 3 Function Points, applies.

↪ Update Calendar Data (**Save**)—EI
We can update data for an existing calendar. The resulting count for this EI would be less than 16 DETs and 1 FTR. If we look at the matrices for applying the weights we see that a value of Low, or 3 Function Points, applies.

↪ Calendar—ILF
We are saving information to a calendar file. The resulting count for this ILF would be <20 DETs and 1 RET. If we look at the matrices for applying the weights we see that a value of Low, or 7 Function Points, applies.

Figure 9.4 displays the **Print** function. Appointments may be printed by selecting this entry. A print dialog box appears permitting the selection of "to" and "from" dates for the input side of an EQ. At this point, we can count an EQ for Print Calendar:

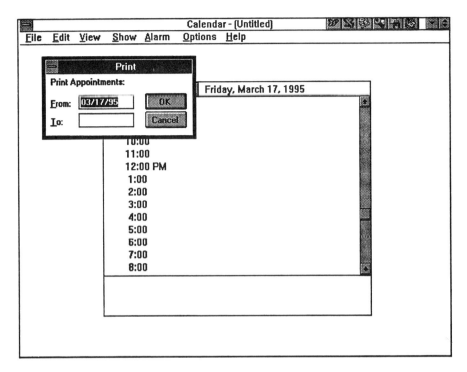

FIGURE 9.4   Microsoft Windows Calendar with Print Selections

↪ **Print** Calendar—EQ

We can select a printed version of our calendar for specified days, not months. There is no derived data. There is a user request, a date retrieval, and a printed display so the transaction is counted as an EQ. The resulting count for this EQ would be less than 20 DETs and 1 FTR on the output side. If we look at the matrices for applying the weights we see that a value of Low, or 3 Function Points, applies.

As we see in Figure 9.5, **Page Setup** permits the selection of headers and footers as well as the margin settings. Figure 9.6 shows **Print Setup** which permits the selection of the printer, paper size, and orientation.

Exit is used for Navigation only.

We can now identify and count these additional selections under the File pull-down menu:

↪ **Page Setup / Print Setup**—EI

Page Setup and Print Setup perform as one function to provide the user the capability to use the default settings from Microsoft Print Manager (an externally maintained file) or to change the settings for this one print job (control

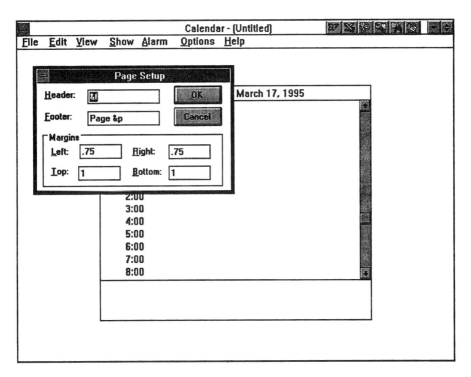

FIGURE 9.5 Microsoft Windows Calendar with Page Setup Selections

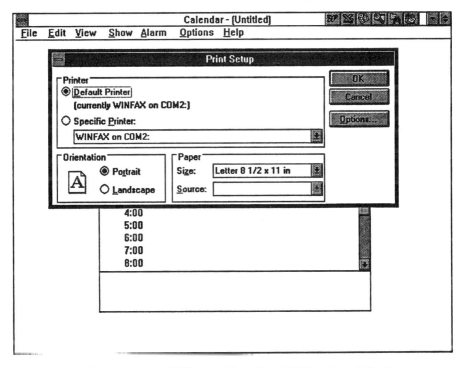

FIGURE 9.6 Microsoft Windows Calendar with Print Setup Selections

data counted as an EI). We can not update Print Manager. The resulting count for this EI would be 5–15 DETs and 1 FTR. If we look at the matrices for applying the weights we see that a value of Low, or 3 Function Points, applies.

↪ **Print Manager—EIF**
Information is retrieved from Print Manager. The resulting count for this EIF would be <20 DETs and 1 RET. If we look at the matrices for applying the weights we see that a value of Low, or 5 Function Points, applies.

↪ **Exit**
Navigation only; not counted.

Figure 9.7 displays the **Edit** option.

↪ Cut, Copy, and Paste
Cut, Copy, and **Paste** are Windows tools. These functions are not considered to be additional functionality provided within Calendar.

↪ **Remove** (Delete)—EI
This function (shown in Figure 9.8) permits the deletion of the appointments for one or more calendar dates. The resulting count for this EI would be <5

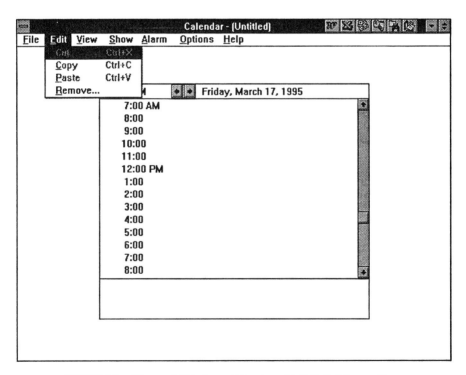

FIGURE 9.7   Microsoft Windows Calendar with Edit Pull-Down Menu

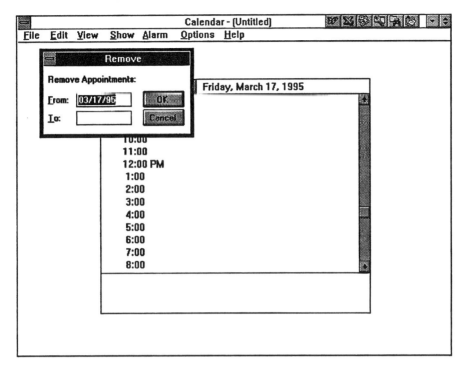

FIGURE 9.8   Microsoft Windows Calendar with Remove Selections

DETs and 1 FTR. If we look at the matrices for applying the weights we see that a value of Low, or 3 Function Points, applies.

View (Figure 9.9) permits the retrieval of daily or monthly views:

⇨ **View Day**
This function permits the display of a day's calendar. This was already counted with Calendar Open.

⇨ **View Month—EQ**
Permits the display of a month's calendar (as shown in Figure 9.10). The resulting count for this EQ would be less than 20 DETs and 1 FTR on the output side. If we look at the matrices for applying the weights we see that a value of Low, or 3 Function Points, applies.

⇨ **Show (Today, Previous, Next)**
Figure 9.11 displays this choice. This is part of the input side of the two EQs for day and month. It is not separate functionality but counted with the view selections. Someone could argue that **Previous/Next** might provide additional

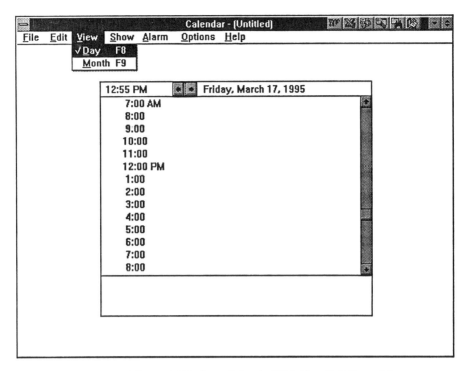

FIGURE 9.9 Microsoft Windows Calendar With View Pull-Down Menu

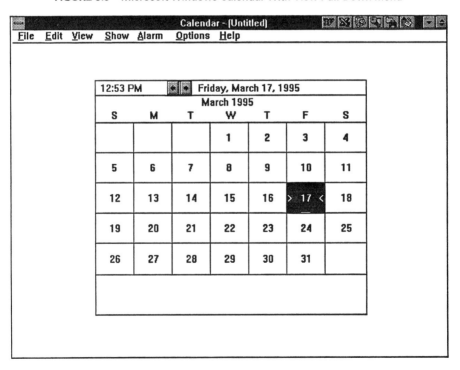

FIGURE 9.10 Microsoft Windows Calendar with View-Month Display

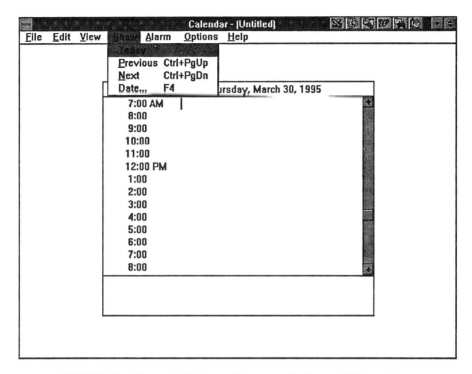

FIGURE 9.11   Microsoft Windows Calendar with Show Pull-Down Menu

functionality as either a control EI or and additional EQ. Our position is that this functionality should be considered navigational.

Show (Figure 9.11) provides the control aspects of the **View** selection. Users can select **Today,** the **Previous,** or **Next** day or month or a specific **Date:**

↪ **Show Date—EQ**
As shown in Figure 9.12, this is an additional logical manner of selecting a particular date and may be counted as a separate EQ. It works on its own as opposed to being related to the Open Calendar function. The resulting count for this EQ would be less than 20 DETs and 1 FTR on the output side. If we look at the matrices for applying the weights we see that a value of Low, or 3 Function Points, applies.

Alarm provides the options of **Set** (Figure 9.13). The alarm may be set or removed by selecting time. Obviously, the alarm displays and can be turned off. We count this functionality as follows:

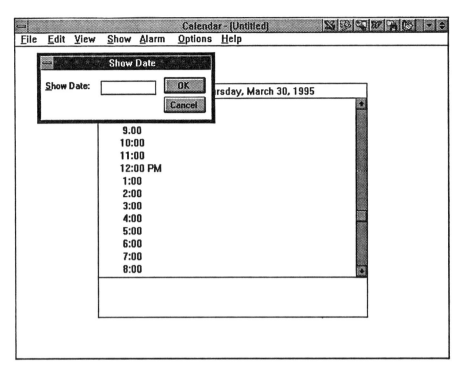

FIGURE 9.12 Microsoft Windows Calendar with Show Date Selections

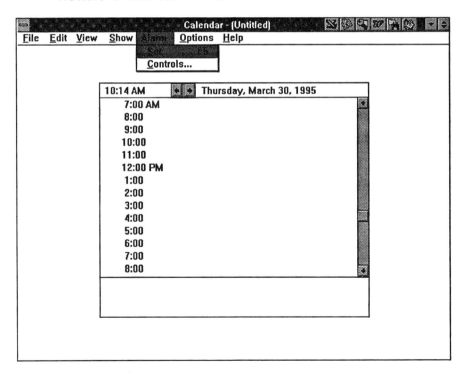

FIGURE 9.13 Microsoft Windows Calendar with Alarm Pull-Down Menu

↪ **Set/Remove Alarm—EI**
The capability of setting/removing an alarm for a particular time and date should be counted as an EI. We save this information to the previously counted calendar file. The resulting count for this EI would be 1–4 DETs and 1 FTR. If we look at the matrices for applying the weights we see that a value of Low, or 3 Function Points applies.

Controls (Figure 9.14) provide set-up for **Alarm**, including selection of silent alarm and early ring. We count this additional functionality as follows:

↪ **Alarm Controls —EI**
We make and save selections for alarm controls. The resulting count for this EI would be 1–4 DETs and 1 FTR. If we look at the matrices for applying the weights we see that a value of Low, or 3 Function Points, applies.

↪ **Alarm Controls—ILF**
Our Alarm Controls selections do not relate directly to a particular date and time, so they are saved to a different file. The resulting count for this ILF would be <20 DETs and 1 RET. If we look at the matrices for applying the weights we see that a value of Low, or 7 Function Points, applies.

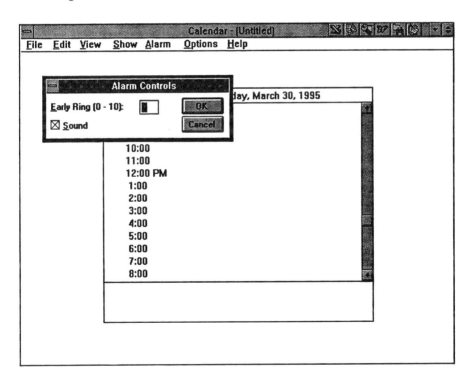

FIGURE 9.14   Microsoft Windows Calendar with Alarm Controls Selections

↩ **Alarm—EO**
Obviously, the alarm goes off at the designated times. The resulting count for this EO would be 1–5 DETs and 2 FTRs. If we look at the matrices for applying the weights we see that a value of Low, or 4 Function Points, applies.

↩ **Alarm Acknowledgment—EI**
The alarm must be turned off. The resulting count for this EI would be 1–4 DETs and 1 FTR. If we look at the matrices for applying the weights we see that a value of Low, or 3 Function Points, applies.

Options (Figure 9.15) give the choice of **Mark, Special Time,** and **Day Setting.**

↩ **Mark—EI**
We can mark a date within the calendar with up to five specific symbols (Figure 9.16). The resulting count for this EI would be 5–15 DETs and 1 FTR. If we look at the matrices for applying the weights we see that a value of Low, or 3 Function Points, applies.

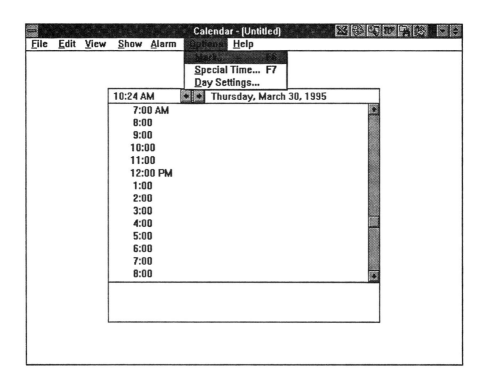

FIGURE 9.15 Microsoft Windows Calendar with Options Pull-Down Menu

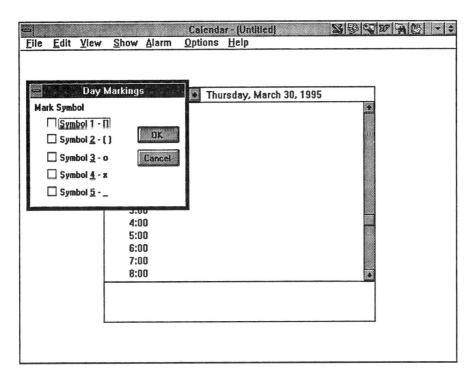

FIGURE 9.16   Microsoft Windows Calendar with Mark Selections

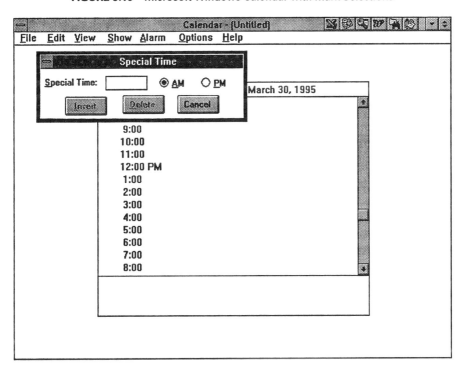

FIGURE 9.17   Microsoft Windows Calendar with Special Time Selections

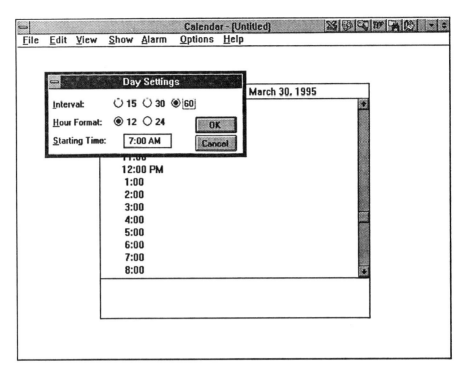

FIGURE 9.18 Microsoft Windows Calendar with Day Settings Selections

⇰ **Special Time—EI**
We can either enter/delete a specific time on our calendar (Figure 9.17). This is an update function, not separate add and delete functions. The resulting count for this EI would be 1–4 DETs and 1 FTR. If we look at the matrices for applying the weights we see that a value of Low, or 3 Function Points, applies.

⇰ **Day Settings—EI**
Similar to the special time function, we can modify our calendar to provide different intervals and starting times (Figure 9.18). Appointment settings can be set in 15, 30, or 60 minute intervals and based upon a 12 or 24 hour format. Starting time may be revised. The resulting count for this EI would be 1–4 DETs and 1 FTR. If we look at the matrices for applying the weights we see that a value of Low, or 3 Function Points, applies.

Determine the Unadjusted Function Point Count. The Unadjusted Function Point count is computed from the sum of all the data and transaction function types (see Table 9.1).

TABLE 9.1 Unadjusted Function Point Count for Microsoft Windows Calendar

Function Types	Low	Average	High	Total
External Inputs	10×3	$\times 6$	2×6	30
External Outputs	2×4	$\times 5$	$\times 7$	8
External Inquiries	4×3	$\times 4$	$\times 6$	12
Internal Logical Files	2×7	$\times 10$	$\times 15$	14
External Interface Files	2×5	$\times 7$	$\times 10$	10
			Total Unadjusted Function Points (UFPs) = 74	

Determine The Value Adjustment Factor of the Fourteen General System Characteristics (Table 9.2).

TABLE 9.2 General Systems Characteristics for Microsoft Windows Calendar

Characteristic	Degree of Influence	Characteristic	Degree of Influence
1. Data Communications	4	8. Online Update	3
2. Distributed Factors	0	9. Complex Processing	1
3. Performance	3	10. Reuseability	2
4. Heavily Used Configuration	2	11. Installation Ease	1
5. Transaction Rate	3	12. Operational Ease	3
6. Online Data Entry	5	13. Multiple Site	2
7. End User Efficiency	4	14. Facilitate Change	2
		Total Degree of Influence = 35	

Calculate The Final Adjusted Function Point Count. Our Final Function Point count for the installed application is determined from the Value Adjustment Factor and the Unadjusted Function Point count:

$$\text{Value Adjustment Factor (VAF)} = .65 + (.01 \times \text{TDI}) = 1.00$$
$$\text{Final Function Point Count (FP)} = \text{UFP} \times \text{VAF}$$

$$\text{Final Function Point Count} = 74 \times 1.00 = 74$$

CHAPTER

10

ACCURATE ESTIMATING

INTRODUCTION

Software practitioners have been challenged to accurately estimate software projects since the early use of computers. It speaks poorly of the software community as a business entity that the issue of accurate estimating has not been adequately addressed and standardized. This chapter will address the use of a basic estimating model and the utilization of Function Points as one of its key components. The estimating principles are expressed in a simplistic fashion. We do not intend to convey the notion that proper estimating is simple or effortless. Good estimating requires skill, commitment, and resources. Our intent in this chapter is to demonstrate the value of the Function Point methodology in properly estimating and managing a project. Table 10.1 characterizes the barriers to successful estimation.

If a project is not adversely affected by one of the situations mentioned in Table 10.1, poor project management is the only excuse for not being able to estimate consistently and accurately. In short, if we understand and are familiar with the problem domain and we understand the environment in which we are developing, then we should be able to predict the outcome.

TABLE 10.1 Barriers to Accurate Estimating

Area	Problem	Detail
Familiarization	Required functionality is not well understood	The analysts are unfamiliar with the functionality required to meet the desired business need.
Change	Changing scope of work	The functionality is well understood; however, frequent or substantive changes in scope are being introduced during the development effort.
Knowledge	Unfamiliar with technology	The tools, techniques, methods, or technology, with which we are involved, are unfamiliar.

THE ESTIMATING MODEL

The elements of our estimating model shown in Figure 10.1 consist of *functional size, complexity,* and *influencers.* These three components, when factored together, result in the desired estimates. By applying this model in the context of the example of building a house, we may better understand the interaction of the components of the model.

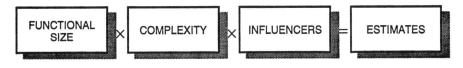

FIGURE 10.1 A Basic Estimating Model

As consumers (users) we are interested in building a new house (application). We know conceptually what we want and we take our requirements to the contractor (developer). The contractor asks us many questions regarding the number, type, and size of rooms we want: bedrooms, kitchen, den, dining room, living room, etc. At this stage of the process the contractor has knowledge regarding the **functional size** we desire. Within our software problem domain, we too must understand the required functionality. Here is where we use

Function Points to examine and understand the inputs, outputs, inquiries, and files to be used in satisfying the user request.

Next we review details about utilities, fixtures, flooring, wall coverings, etc. These are detailed features that will add to the overall complexity of the basic plans. We may have asked for a living room, but when we reviewed this requirement in greater detail with the developer, we reveal that we want a sunken living room with track lighting and built-in book shelves. The

original square footage or functionality of our house is the same, but there certainly is an added **complexity** that must be considered when we build this particular room. So too with our software solution. We have calculated the size expressed in inputs, outputs, inquiries, etc., but there are additional complexities that need to be considered. The answer is the Function Point General Systems Characteristics (GSCs). These fourteen factors take into consideration those additional variables that are part of the requirements but were not directly accounted for in the data and transaction function types. For example, a system requirement may identify the need for a particular type of input transaction. It may also be requested that this particular input be delivered in an on-line environment with a high degree of user friendliness for data entry. The Function Point methodology does not assume that all function types are to be treated equally and therefore uses the GSCs to determine added complexity based on our user's requirements.

Finally, the contractor draws up a set of plans (functional design). We review these plans, and agree that this is the house (system) we want. The next step is for the contractor to give us an estimate as to how long it will take and what it will cost to build our house.

During his estimating process the contractor will factor in the functional size of the work product and its level of complexity. He has built many homes in the past and has a good baseline of experience on which to base his estimates. However, there are still other considerations that he must bring into play when estimating. He will need to consider such things as how much skilled labor is available to help on this project, what opportunities exist for using auto- mated tools (e.g., automated hammers) in the building process, and what physical environmental factors might be encountered where he intends to build the house. There are many **influencers** that he must consider before completing his estimate.

> INFLUENCERS

Finally, he completes the cost and delivery estimate. We are comfortable with the estimate because we have participated in the process, and the builder has demonstrated an understanding of what we functionally require. We are working with an experienced builder, who has done this many times before, and we can expect the actual cost and delivery to be within +/– 5% of his original estimate.

Getting back to our systems environment, we can readily see how these principles and estimating practices would apply to meeting our need to accurately define a software work product. The role of the Function Point methodology in this process is critical. The Function Point method satisfies our need to accurately evaluate two of the three estimating model components: size and complexity (Figure 10.2).

Functional Size is based upon the accurate evaluation of the Transaction and Data Function Types. The *complexity* is the result of the assessment of the fourteen General System Characteristics. The *influencers* are those variables that influence the development effort.

In an earlier chapter we discussed these same influencers in the context of qualitative data. We said they included such things as the software processes that

Function Points

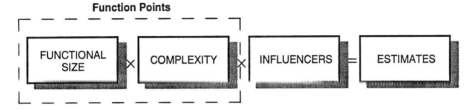

FIGURE 10.2   Function Points as Part of the Estimating Model

we will be utilizing on any given project, the skill levels of the staff that are involved in the project (including user personnel), the level of automation that we can
bring to bear on the effort, and the influences of the business environment; for example, competition and regulatory requirements. In fact there are numerous factors
that influence our ability to deliver software in a timely fashion with high quality.
Table 10.2 displays a number of influencing factors, in six categories, that must be
evaluated in order to produce an accurate estimate.

Similar to our example of the contractor and his baseline of experience, as
software developers we too will need to build a baseline of experience with regard
to the performance of these factors across different projects and types of applications. We need to develop profiles that we can use as templates in our estimating
model.

In Chapter 2 we discussed baselining. During a baselining process we develop
a quantitative base of performance levels based on product size. Along with those

TABLE 10.2   Estimating Influence Factors

Management	Definition	Design
➤ Team Dynamics	➤ Clearly Stated Requirements	➤ Formal Process
➤ High Morale	➤ Formal Process	➤ Rigorous Reviews
➤ Project Tracking	➤ Customer Involvement	➤ Design Reuse
➤ Project Planning	➤ Experience Levels	➤ Customer Involvement
➤ Automation	➤ Busness Impact	➤ Experienced Development Staff
➤ Management Skills		➤ Automation

Build	Test	Environment
➤ Code Reviews	➤ Formal Testing Methods	➤ New Technology
➤ Source Code Tracking	➤ Test Plans	➤ Automated Process
➤ Code Reuse	➤ Development Staff Experience	➤ Adequate Training
➤ Data Administration	➤ Effective Test Tools	➤ Organizational Dynamics
➤ Computer Availability	➤ Customer Involvement	➤ Certification
➤ Experienced Staff		
➤ Automation		

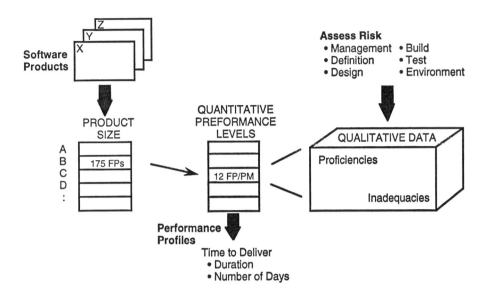

FIGURE 10.3   Developing Baseline Profiles

quantitative performance levels we have collected qualitative data from individual assessments of risk factors. For each project assessed, we have gathered information with regard to the factors that influenced the quantitative results based upon specific proficiencies and inadequacies. From this sampling we can develop a set of performance profiles (Figure 10.3) which can be used as templates for future estimating.

Accurate estimating is a function of applying a process and recognizing that that effort must be expended in creating a baseline of experience that will allow for increased accuracy of that process. Estimating does not require a crystal ball; it simply requires a commitment.

Thus far we have been working in an environment where all the variables are known and predictable. Let's now reintroduce those three barriers to successful estimating discussed earlier: familiarization, change, and knowledge. What do we do when one or more of these elements are introduced into our environment?

Familiarization

If we are assigned a problem that is ill-defined, or we lack the experience to fully understand the problem, then naturally it will be difficult to accurately estimate what it will take to successfully solve that problem. If our contractor is faced with building a new type of roof that he has no prior experience with, then he will not be favorably positioned to give us an accurate estimate. At least two reasonable options are available in this situation. First we can build models (prototyping) that simulate the situation. From this experience we can estimate the real job or continue to operate in a prototyping mode until we have gained control over the scope of work. Secondly we can look for the knowledge outside our immediate domain. Perhaps some other organization, either internal or external, has had experience in this particular area and can provide us with insight as to the scope of work. With the exception of leading-edge projects, once the situation is recognized, there should be limited impact on a project deliverable because of a lack of familiarity.

Change

Changes in scope are a common and necessary occurrence. The use of Function Points once again lends itself effectively to managing this often problematic situation. With a simple example, we can readily see how effective the Function Point technique can be.

Our original project estimate was 300 Function Points. Due to changes in the requirements, a subsequent estimate reveals that the project has increased by 50 Function Points (Figure 10.4). Assuming that we know our rate of delivery from our baseline data, we can accurately estimate what the impact of the change will be.

	Original Estimate	Current Estimate	Variance
Function Points	300	350	+50

FIGURE 10.4   Comparing Current and Original Estimates

Because we have used the Function Point counting methodology we can readily assess what those 50 additional Function Points are based on. Furthermore, we can express this change in scope in terms our user can understand. The increase of 50 Function Points was the result of on-line screen changes and additional reporting requirements. Using our baseline data we can predict additional effort, schedule, and costs (Figure 10.5).

Change in Scope	Resulting Count	Additional Effort (Staff Months)	Additional Costs ($000)	Added Schedule Time
On-line Screen Changes	30	1.5	15	.3
Report Additions	20	1	10	.2
Total	50	2.5	$25	.5 months

FIGURE 10.5   Assessing the Impact of Added Functionality

Knowledge

As new tools, techniques, and methods are introduced, they will influence our ability to accurately estimate work efforts. Once again we may not have a baseline upon which to base our estimates. We must take advantage of some base of knowledge that already exists until we develop our own. This may be an opportunity to use industry data. We may be able to draw from industry experiences to develop a rough estimate.

The industry data in Figure 10.6 depicts what would be required for a distributed system project of 800 Function Points, based on industry norms. The delivery rate of 8 Function Points per person month can then be applied to compute the number of resources we will require. More appropriately we can use this value to determine a project cost based upon person months of effort. Function Points do not serve as a resource scheduler. What we know from this estimate is that we will require 100 person months of effort. We then need to use other techniques and tools to determine how we will staff and schedule the work load.

Let's summarize what we have learned:

↝ Function Point methodology is a key component of the estimating model. It allows us to accurately size the software problem. Because Function Point counting is a learned process that can be applied consistently, an organization can expect to obtain accurate sizing from its project managers.

↝ Function Points do not serve as a crystal ball. If requirements are not adequately stated, or cannot be determined through a rigorous definition process, then there is little hope to accurately size the deliverable.

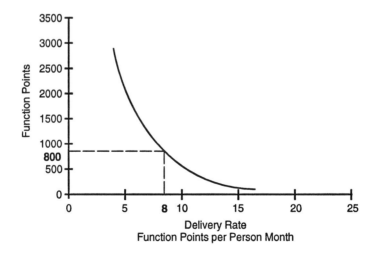

FIGURE 10.6   Using Industry Benchmark Data to Predict Delivery Rate

↪ Function Points measure the functionality being delivered. When there is a shift in that functional deliverable (change in scope), the Function Point method is the best means to rescope the size. It also has value in the fact that it is expressing the change in scope in terms that the user can understand.

↪ Function Point data, such as industry benchmarks, can be an effective enabler to improving estimating accuracy.

11

SUCCESS STORIES

INTRODUCTION

There are a wide variety of business experiences involving the successful application of the Function Point techniques described in this book. Admittedly, there are probably an equal number of experiences involving functional metrics that could be cited as failures. Our focus is to put a more positive spin on the whole notion of software measurement. We acknowledge the painful failures, but we offer hope based upon the numerous successes that we have witnessed.

We have selected four success stories to share with you. For the most part, these experiences represent typical consulting engagements. They have their different twists and turns, with successful and not so successful results. These particular stories were chosen based upon their diverse and successful use of function points and software measurement. Not all are from our client base, so we take no credit for the successes. We simply wanted to share some experiences from which we all can learn.

RDI

RDI is a ten year old commercial software developer. The primary mission of RDI is the production of PC software products. On time, on budget, commercial quality software is the goal of RDI's process-oriented development environment. RDI develops software for a wide range of client needs from traditional business applications to graphical programming tools for the automated control of industrial and commercial equipment. The following text is a summary of a presentation given at the 1994 IFPUG conference in Orlando, FL. Ken Florian, president of RDI, gave the presentation, which was very well received.

Introduction

RDI's presentation focused on how the company extends Function Point analysis to the realm of contracting and formal pricing of a software development project. RDI began using Function Point analysis approximately three years ago. Two years ago they developed the concept of Function Point Budgeting. Function Point Budgeting was developed in order to responsibly and professionally charge for software development services. RDI uses Function Point analysis for the critical activities of cost and schedule estimating because Function Point analysis is objective, repeatable, and understandable.

RDI notes that their clients don't purchase lines of code; they purchase software functionality that serves specific business needs. Function Point analysis allows end-users and developers to share a common dialogue about the size and cost of a system in the only measurement that really matters—functionality.

Background

Software developers are constantly faced with the challenge of providing accurate quotations for software development projects. Analysis and programming are both an art and a science, and productivity is extremely variable among both analysts and programmers.

The default method for sizing software projects has been to rely upon the developer's experience to compute a "ball park" estimate for the project. Depending upon the developer's estimating and application development experience and the complexity of the project, estimates can be off by 20% or more. With large-scale, highly complex projects, it is possible for estimates to be off by as much as 200%.

Once satisfied that the project estimate is as accurate as possible, the developer must communicate the estimate to the customer. This means presenting the estimated cost of the project to the customer in a manner that will maximize the customer's comfort level and set the customer's expectations while minimizing the developer's risk. Traditionally, the form of presentation takes one of two formats: time and materials or fixed price.

Before we proceed to analyze the pitfalls of these two forms of pricing, let's review a fundamental principal associated with software pricing. To measure software in Function Points is to think about software in terms of the number of functional units. Function Point analysis answers the question, "How many of these things (software functions) are there in this system?" Once we have the size in Function Point units, we can think about a cost per unit.

Pricing Methods

We will now look at three pricing methods and demonstrate how number of units apply and are related to each pricing method.

Time and Materials. With a time and materials pricing method, the client is required to absorb two risks:

1. They must absorb the risk for how large a software deliverable they want. From simple requests (for example, name changes) to complex requests (for example, real-time financial transactions), the client decides what they require to meet their business needs.
2. The client also absorbs the risk for the cost per unit. A unit in this case represents an "hour" of a person's time. Using the time and materials approach, the developer states the estimated cost and makes best efforts to keep the project within the original budget. The customer pays for each hour worked based on an agreed hourly rate. There may or may not be a maximum specified. Typically, if the project goes over budget, there are contractual provisions for handling the situation, to the extreme of canceling the project.

This means that the client absorbs the total risk for the developer's competency. If the project manager chooses to use unskilled labor, then the cost will very likely be higher than if experienced staff were used. While the developer and client may have a "mutual understanding" of the approximate budget in a time and materials project, in a true time and materials project the final cost to the client is unknown and unknowable up front.

This pricing method is not conducive to a long-term relationship with the client. Eventually, the developer will underestimate a project and the customer will exceed the budget or, worse, cancel the project. It is a lose-lose approach.

Fixed-Price. In a fixed price approach, the software developer absorbs both the risk for cost and the number of units (the size of the software requested by the client). The developer will typically build into the fixed price quotation a large contingency amount to cover the risk.

There are two problems with this approach. First the contingency built into the quotation erodes the value/price ratio because the developer is increasing the price by a specific amount for an unknown amount of future creep, and then the customer may reject the quote as being too expensive. Second, once a fixed-price quotation is accepted, no matter how well "spec'ed" a system, there is inevitably "function creep". The entire risk of under-estimation is placed on the developer.

At some point during the project, there is likely to be a situation where the customer and the developer are not in agreement as to what is included in the functionality of the software deliverable. The developer may use the requirements as the basis for argument, and the customer may counter with a statement suggesting that for all the money they are paying, additional features should be included.

At this point, the developer is in a predicament. The developer wants the company to be happy (after all, reputation and repeat business opportunities are at stake). The developer also wants to maintain at least a remote chance of making a profit. Despite the potential for incurring a significant cost increase, the developer often will avoid a dispute and write off the extra work to goodwill.

Sometimes, extended feature creep can end up doubling the developer's cost, which really strains the relationship. In this situation, a developer will probably insist that all future business be on a time and materials basis. This is also a lose-lose approach.

Function Point Budgeting. RDI believes that the best way to reduce the estimation risk is to establish a "Function Point Budget." This is done by distributing the two risks: (1) number of units measured in Function Points and (2) cost per unit, measured in dollars, where they belong. The client should be wholly responsible for the size of the software they request, design, and fund. The developer should be wholly responsible up front (at the time of contract signing and before any development work is started) for the cost per unit. This is a win-win solution.

RDI maintains a historical baseline of measured data which includes, by project, Function Point counts on finished software, RDI's real cost per Function Point, total cost, and language used. This information is used during the cost and schedule estimating process on subsequent projects. For the new project, a Function Point count is developed and a cost per Function Point quote is stated based upon the various count ranges. Throughout the project (as changes occur), RDI repeats the Function Point counting and reports the status to the customer. If the project is under budget, the customer can choose to pay less or to add features and increase the functionality. If the project is over budget, the customer can decide to pay more or to remove features and decrease the functionality.

Contractual Expression of Function Point Budgeting

After initial analysis, a joint decision is made regarding the size of the finished product. The contractual schedule commitment and costs are based on this size. The Function Point count becomes a "functional budget" for the software which the client can "spend." If the client decides, during design, that a new feature is needed, something else must be sacrificed to keep within the Function Point budget, or the budget must be increased.

During the course of design and development, the Function Point count is frequently updated. If our client decides that the overall size of the project must increase, a new Function Point budget is established, the new cost is taken from the table in the contract, and a new schedule is prepared for the revised larger project.

Sample

RDI agrees to complete a contract at a fixed price per Function Point. The current system size is 2,247 Function Points. As a reference guide, the cost per Function Point is displayed in Table 11.1. Pricing is based on size ranges expressed in Function Point count values. RDI applies these costs based on a breakdown of the total Function Point size by price range. For example, if a client has a requirement that is assessed at 2,000 Function Points the cost would be $967 per Function Point. If they added 10 additional Function Points the cost would then jump to $1,019 per Function Point; this would obviously be viewed unfavorably by the client. Instead, RDI assesses the first 2000 Function Points at the $967 rate and the 10 additional Function Points at $1,019 rate. Applying this costing structure to our current example of 2,247 Function Points we would compute a total cost of $2,185,693. The first 2000 Function Points at $967 equals $1,934,000 and the additional 247 Function Points at $1,019 equal $251,693. The amount is paid according to the payment schedule which is attached as an integral part of the contract. RDI and the client agree to reevaluate the payment schedule at Functional Design sign-off.

Functional Design Charges. The system is counted at the conclusion of functional design. This count is based on a formal sign-off by the client on the functional design documentation. This count is the Functional Design Count. Using the Functional Design Count, the charges for the functional design are calculated using the following equation:

Functional Design Count × Functional Design Cost per Function Point
at the cost for the Functional Design Count = charges

TABLE 11.1   Function Point Pricing Table

Function Point Count	Functional Design Cost Per Function Point	Inplementation Cost Per Function Point	Total Cost Per Function Point
1,501–2,000	$242	$725	$967
2,001–2,501	$255	$764	$1,019
2,501–3,000	$265	$793	$1,058
3,001–3500	$274	$820	$1,094
3,501–4,000	$284	$850	$1,134

Implementation Charges. Implementation includes engineering, coding, integration, and testing. The total Function Point count of the portions of the functional design selected by the client for implementation is the Baseline Count. At the conclusion of development, the completed software is counted. This count is the Net Final Count. The charges for implementation are calculated using the following equation:

(Baseline Count × Implementation Cost per Function Point
at the cost for the Net Final Count) + (Function Points added, changed,
or deleted during implementation × Total Cost per Function Point
at the cost for the Net Final Count) = Charges for Implementation

Conclusion

Function Point analysis and budgeting provides the best objective method for sizing software projects and for managing the size of a software project during development. It is the best method for managing risk because the client accepts the risk for the size of the software project requested (the Function Point count) and the developer accepts the risk for the cost of production (the cost per Function Point). Adherence to methodical Function Point counting optimizes the client-developer relationship, and facilitates on-time, on-budget software development projects.

U.S. NAVY

The following are excerpts from the Naval Surface Warfare Center report, NAVSWC TR 91-715, authored by Paul Lusher, December 1991.

Introduction

This report documents an effort to research and evaluate methods to measure, predict, and improve the productivity of software development projects. The approach is to measure the software development quality and productivity of a completed project as a way to "baseline" the current software development process within the Gun Fire Control Systems Branch (G72). In order to increase quality and productivity, weaknesses must be identified in the current methods and then steps must be taken to strengthen these areas of the software development process. To accomplish this, a baseline measurement of the factors that influence quality and productivity must be defined. This report also discusses various "software metrics", i.e., measurements of software deliverables (requirements and source code metrics) and of the project itself (project metrics such as effort in person-months, cost, and schedule). These measurements are used to provide better up-front estimation of software development projects. Therefore, this report encompasses two basic thrusts: 1) better project estimation via collection of software metrics, and 2) improvements to the software development process via self-evaluation and the establishment of a baseline of current development processes.

This baseline report measures the current software development process used to develop the DDG-51 Gun Weapon System computer programs. This development project was performed by the Software Engineering Group within G72. The work documented in this report was performed as part of a Weapons Control Division initiative to improve the software development processes for various Weapons Control projects.

Background

This software development baseline measurement was performed by analyzing the computer programs that make up the Gun Computer System MK-160 Mod 4 (GCS). This system is part of the Gun Weapon System MK-34 (GWS) consisting of the GCS, a Gun Mount, and the associated ammunition. This is a newly developed GWS for the DDG-51 class of AEGIS destroyers. The lead ship in this class, the USS Arleigh Burke, was commissioned July 4, 1991. The GCS software development work was basically performed from 1983 to 1988, with maintenance and fleet support work ongoing to date.

The GCS is basically comprised of two separate computers (and associated computer programs), operator consoles for each computer, and tape drives. The two computers are referred to as the Gun Console Computer (GCC) and the Gun Mount Processor (GMP), each a standard AN/UYK-44 16-bit mini-computer. Refer to Figure 11.1 for a system diagram.

Methodology

The baseline process approach was to baseline organizational software development productivity by measuring completed software development projects. This baseline is then used to determine which development process improvements may be the most cost effective. It is compared with future projects so that productivity gains may be identified. Productivity, in general, is defined as the amount of "system functionality" (in Function Points) that is produced per unit time.

The Function Point count is a requirements-level software metric that measures the functionality to be provided by a given system (see Appendix for detailed count values). It can be computed during the requirements analysis phase of a project. This gives an approximate measurement of the functionality to be delivered from the viewpoint of the user. Most importantly, Function Points remove the system sizing issue from the implementation dependent coding phase of the project. Given a requirements specification (a system specification or Prime Item Development Specification, or better still, a Program Performance Specification or System Requirement Specification) and the associated Interface Definition Specifications (IDS or IRS), one can estimate the number of Function Points contained in the given set of requirements. This provides an up-front system size estimate in terms that relate to user interests (functional requirements) better than the traditional Lines-of-Code estimate. No attempt is made in this report to completely define Function Point counting rules. Other software metrics used to measure the software development process include Lines-of-Code and project/productivity metrics (actual project results) such as total effort (in person months), cost, calendar schedule, and number of defects.

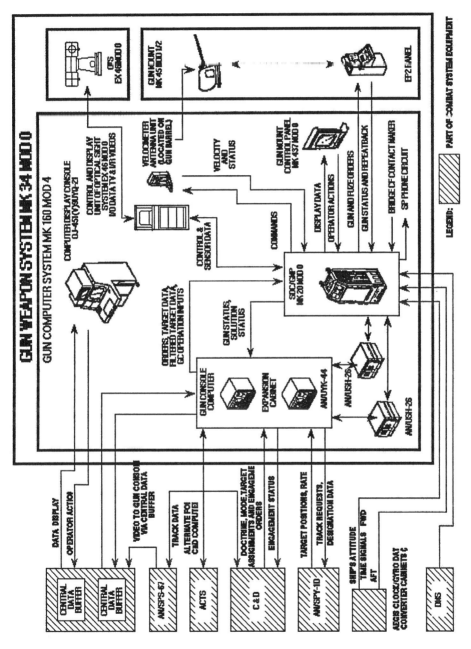

FIGURE 11.1 Gun Computer System Diagram

153

Recommendations

As a result of the GCS software development baseline process, two sets of recommendations have been developed. The first set suggests improvements in the software development process that evolved from the soft factor evaluation performed as part of the baseline process.

The second set of recommendations is in the area of project metric data collection. The attempt to collect actual project results metric data for the GCS development made clear the fact that such documentation is usually nonexistent and is very difficult to reconstruct after the fact. In particular, effort and staffing data, broken down by software development phase, is required for evaluating project development but is not readily available.

Software Development Process Improvements

In considering improvements in the software development process, recommendations were limited to those areas that have some chance of actually being changed. Therefore, the area of environment was not addressed. Weaknesses such as office environment, speed/memory restrictions, program execution frequency, and novel hardware/functions cannot readily be changed. Indeed, the nature of real-time, embedded weapon systems development will always dictate most of these environmental limits on productivity. Similarly, personnel weaknesses such as project organization structure (matrix management), project management methods and experience, and user involvement during testing either have changed already or are not likely to change. However, a number of improvements were recommended in the area of software development technology and process.

Summary and Conclusions

It is recognized that software quality drives productivity; i.e., in order to increase productivity, there must be an increase in the quality of the software under production. This follows from the inordinate amount of time and money usually expended in redesign of faulty software and in the testing and maintenance phases of a project to remove software defects. When fewer defects are created or more defects are found earlier in project phases, less time is spent producing a system. Therefore, project productivity is increased as quality increases. In order to increase quality and productivity, weaknesses must be identified in the methods currently used and steps taken to strengthen these areas of our software development process. To accomplish this, factors must first be measured—the ones that influence productivity. Thus, it will be possible to identify those areas which can benefit most from improvement. Using project measurements as the guide, the software development processes can be improved throughout the Weapons Control Division.

Measurement is a prerequisite for improvement. Only by knowing where the software development process stands can changes to the process be made and demonstrations developed to show the improvement. Awareness of the necessity for measurement and the application of the various software metrics to project estimation is an initial step toward a more quantitative approach to software development. This study is intended to begin this process and to educate members of the G72 Software Engineering Group, and the entire Weapons Control Division, regarding software metrics and their use in estimating and controlling software projects. The experience of collecting past project metric data on the GCS development made clear the necessity of ongoing data collection.

Measurement of system functionality at the requirements phase using Function Points was reasonably successful. The method has some ambiguity and depends somewhat on interpretation, but a requirements phase sizing method is essential for accurate project estimation. Studies by the International Function Point Users Group indicate there can be a plus-or-minus 15% variation in Function Point counts of the same system done by experienced counters. However, this is more accurate than counts of Lines-of-Code during system definition work when project estimates are needed. Furthermore, it is more appealing on a philosophical level to measure system functionality versus source code. Systems deliver functionality to users, not lines of programming language; users, in general, do not care about the source code, but do care about the job the system is built to perform. System sizing must eventually be removed from the implementation dependent domain of actual source code.

The after-the-fact estimates of the GCS development using Function Points and an estimating tool (Checkpoint) were fairly close to the actual project results. They were certainly better than many traditional estimates seen on past projects. The Function Point count for these two applications are provided in Appendix G.

TRANSQUEST (AT&T/DELTA)

January 1, 1995, AT&T Global Information Solutions (AT&T) and Delta Air Lines (Delta) formed a 50/50 joint venture partnership called TransQuest Information Solutions (TransQuest). In addition to the fifty year joint venture agreement, Delta has signed a ten year services agreement with TransQuest with an estimated value of $2.8 billion.

Introduction

Our first introduction to this engagement was based on a request from AT&T to support its efforts in determining current software development and maintenance performance levels at Delta that could be used as the basis for establishing contractual improvement targets.

The provider of services (in this case TransQuest) is contracting to deliver and support application software over the term of the service agreement. Improvements in targeted rate of delivery and level of support (resulting in price-performance improvements) over the life of the contract, which were mutually agreeable to both parties, needed to be established. Delta required a way to ensure that it was receiving the promised benefit, and AT&T wanted to ensure that improvements achieved were calculable.

A Function Point baseline study was the method used to quantify and establish productivity levels. This approach establishes current performance levels relative to the amount of functionality that is being delivered to the end user and supported by the development group. From this starting point, both parties can agree to the target improvement and associated reduction in cost per Function Point over the life of the contract.

Going forward, both parties have agreed to preestablished and quantifiable levels of service, performance, or rates of improvement. The development group, with a clear understanding of their objectives, is positioned to manage the risk of software development through the use of process assessment techniques and by applying rigorous software metrics. The customer is comfortable with the deliverable since it is being expressed and measured in terms that can readily be understood.

The following discussion is an account of the baseline study that was conducted in the establishment of TransQuest/Delta baseline metrics. The actual results are not revealed but approximations are given to express the nature of the value of the measured results.

Background

The essence of the TransQuest engagement was the establishment of productivity improvement targets that could be clearly expressed in the contract. Function Points methodology was agreed upon as the software unit to be used; cost per Function Point was chosen as the metric to be measured.

The purpose of the Baseline Study focused on two key criteria: obtaining accurate data and producing meaningful results. Obtaining accurate data is important to the success of this study from the standpoint that critical business decisions are based on the resulting analysis of that data. In addition to accuracy of data, the correct data needed to be collected. The objectives of this Baseline Study were

- ⤳ To establish delivery rates for both mainframe and distributed environments
- ⤳ To determine accurate cost per function point based on best data available
- ⤳ To determine performance levels for maintenance
- ⤳ To recommend process improvements

The Baseline Study was preceded by a Risk Impact Profile Study. The results of that study were used to focus the baseline recommendations on appropriate process improvements and critical measures of performance. Following this Baseline Study, activities commenced that included the definition and implementation of practices and processes required to monitor, measure, manage, and improve software development activities.

Baseline Project Approach

The Baseline Study for TransQuest consisted of four major components: *Risk Impact Profile, Delivery Performance, Process Capability* and *Recommendations* (Figure 11.2).

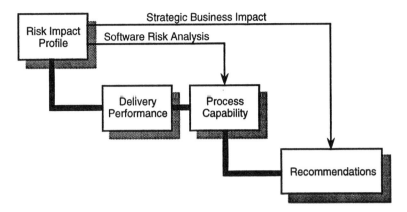

FIGURE 11.2   The Baseline Study Process Flow

Risk Impact Profile.   The Risk Impact Profile resulted in the creation of both a Strategic Business Impact Profile and a Software Risk Analysis Assessment. The Strategic Business Impact Profile assessed numerous related business drivers and highlighted which drivers would be critical to the success of TransQuest. A sample of business drivers evaluated include the following:

↝ Cost Reduction
↝ Improved Delivery Time of Software
↝ Optimization of New Technologies
↝ Standardization of Development Process and Tools
↝ Improved Use of New Methodologies
↝ Increased Technical Skill Levels

The Software Risk Analysis was used to determine which risks were currently incurred in the development of software. Using this perspective, barriers could be identified that would have to be removed in order to successfully meet the business goals as highlighted in the Strategic Business Profile. The characteristics that were examined to identify risks included:

↝ Skills of the Technical Staff
↝ Changing Functionality
↝ Tools, Techniques, and Methods
↝ Requirements Definition Process
↝ Organizational Support Structure

The Risk Impact Profile established the ground work for subsequent baseline establishment activities. It provided high level findings for baseline recommendations and insights into areas of excellence and deficiencies among the various development practices.

Delivery Performance.   Delivery Performance represents the quantitative portion of the Baseline Study. A representative sampling of projects was selected by Delta and AT&T. Data was collected (based on available information) on size of deliverable, level of effort, project duration, number of defects, and cost of each project. These measures were analyzed, and performance levels were established and compared to industry standards. The selection of projects was based on the following selection criteria:

- Completed within last 18 months
- Included development and maintenance
- Included all business areas
- Staffed 50% or greater by Delta personnel
- Took more than 6 staff months to complete
- Were representative of ordinary process
- Included purchased and in-house software
- Included all platforms
- Mix of technologies
- Included all languages

Projects meeting these criteria were then further examined to determine the availability of credible data. The final list included representative projects across all technologies, of various sizes and complexities and across business units.

Each project was sized using the Function Point methodology. Other data including effort, schedule duration, and defects were collected from representative project managers. In some cases, data was not readily available and was recreated through rigorous examination of project activities that had occurred during the life of the project.

Performance levels (expressed as a factor of system size and effort) were computed and graphically displayed. The graphs depicted individual project performance levels, projects specific to the mainframe environment, and projects specific to the distributed environment. There was also a mapping of current industry performance levels in comparison to TransQuest/Delta performance.

From these data points, TransQuest was able to establish accurate targets against which to measure ongoing performance. It also established reasonable expectations with its customers based on historical and factual performance data.

As part of this effort, costs were computed for each project. Following an agreed upon cost model, individual project costs were computed. The result is a Cost per Function Point. Costs included in this calculation included the following:

- Contracted labor wages
- Purchased software packages
- Training
- Development tools
- Staff labor and wages
- Travel expense
- Overhead allocations

Defect data collection and analysis were part of this Baseline Study; however, insufficient data was available to produce a statistically sound result. Delta had not historically tracked defect rates during the development process, and defect information was generally unavailable for test phase activities.

Process Capability.   Process Capability represents the qualitative portion of the Baseline Study. The analysis conducted reveals the influence of current software practices on performance levels. From this assessment it is possible to recommend improvements in current practices, suggest new practices, and emphasize existing practices that have already demonstrated positive influence on productivity.

Data was collected on each project. The method of collection involved lengthy interview/survey sessions with each of the project teams. Data was collected on six key influencing factors: project management, definition, design, build, test, and environment. Individual projects were analyzed, and project profiles were created. This data was also analyzed in aggregate as the basis for developing recommendations.

Recommendations

Three separate and yet related recommendations resulted from this study: recommendations for performance delivery standards, recommendations for process improvement, and recommendations for ongoing measurement practices.

Performance delivery standards will be established as a result of this baseline data. These standards will be the basis for monitoring performance effectiveness and the quality of software deliverables. Process improvement recommendations will focus on those practices that must be improved in order to obtain higher levels of productivity and software quality. Recommendations for ongoing measurement practices will be based on the need to measure the standards established in this baseline; primarily delivery rates and costs.

Conclusion

The results of this study were used to establish the productivity baseline levels and to establish a method to measure improvements in cost and delivery rates in the future. Going forward, both parties will develop in-house expertise to monitor and measure the improvements for comparison to the baseline data.

SAPIENS

Introduction

Sapiens is a Dutch Antilles based company that produces, markets, and sells a Rapid Application Development toolset. It is a multimillion dollar organization with a worldwide client base. It offers products and services in an effort to support client needs to improve the quality of development processes and the abilities to bring products to market in a cost effective and timely fashion.

Background

The Director of Marketing, Dr. Sam Bayer, has been with the company since 1993. He brought to Sapiens the knowledge that software measurement can be effectively applied to understand and improve the development environment. Armed with that knowledge, and wearing his marketing hat, he creatively used software measurement techniques as a marketing vehicle, and in the process also advanced the use of functional metrics. The following techniques represent an overview of the manner in which Sam Bayer, and Sapiens, put metrics analysis to use:

- ⇨ Applying software measurement tools, methods, and techniques to help existing customers gain support within their own companies for the continued use of Sapiens products and services by demonstrating the business benefits they have received
- ⇨ Raising the level of awareness within the marketplace regarding the availability and potential use of software metrics that could be used to aid clients in the purchasing and implementing of software and related tools
- ⇨ Supporting Sapiens' consulting services business in properly setting and managing customer expectations regarding the value they were receiving for their investment
- ⇨ Increasing Sapiens' ability to accurately estimate projects during the bidding process; the resulting value was a win-win situation for both sides
- ⇨ Utilizing software metrics to help strengthen Sapiens' marketing programs; for example, advertising, direct mail
- ⇨ Being able to demonstrate quantitatively, during the sales cycle, to prospective clients that the decision to use Sapiens' products was going to provide benefits to their specific organization based on existing technologies and methodologies employed there

It is these last two items, marketing and sales, that we are going to discuss in greater depth.

Baseline Study Results

Sapiens engaged the services of a highly reputable software measurement consultancy to conduct what is commonly referred to as a Performance Baseline Study. The study was jointly sponsored by Sapiens, IBM, and selected Sapiens clients. Data was collected on selected projects and analyzed to determine levels of software process performance. The results, if favorable, would be published to demonstrate the value of various Sapiens products.

Five sites were selected representing different industries: Telecommunications, Commercial Software, Insurance, Utility, and Manufacturing. A breakdown of the types of systems selected within each industry site follows:

- Telecom—sales and marketing system
- Commercial software—new sales commission system
- Insurance—new remuneration system for agents
- Utility—gas management
- Manufacturing—new order processing system

Several observations can be made regarding the representative sampling. All systems selected represent some form of new development. The importance of this can be significant. With new development projects there is apt to be more accurate data available and more in-house expertise available to answer questions. New development should typically reflect current directions in technologies and system architecture. We can also observe that none of these systems were overly complex in terms of data processing.

The capability baseline process was conducted at each site. Each application was sized using the IFPUG counting guidelines for Function Point analysis. A series of survey questions was presented, and responses were collected for each application. The survey questionnaire collected data regarding software processes that were utilized, skill levels of the software technicians, effectiveness of tools utilized, and involvement of customers. Additionally, level of effort, expressed in person hours, was collected for each project.

The size of projects ranged from a low score of 632 adjusted Function Points to a high of 4519 as depicted in Figure 11.3. The average size of all five projects was 2543. Typical industry size ranges classify systems as average if they fall between a range of 800 to 1200 Function Points, so we are talking about some rather large MIS projects.

Productivity levels were computed using Function Point size and expended level of effort on a per project basis. Productivity levels were compared to industry standards based on Capers Jones industry averages. The computed productivity lev-

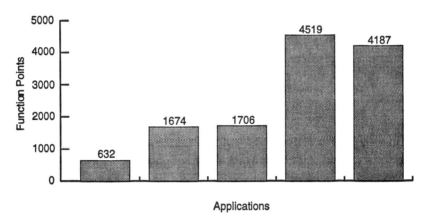

FIGURE 11.3 Application Size Expressed in Function Points

els demonstrate a performance level much higher than industry. When these same projects are compared in Figure 11.4 to more current industry benchmark data, they still show remarkable, positive variances.

Three projects demonstrate a very high productivity rate in comparison to the industry standard. The smallest project did not do quite as well when compared to the industry, but still exceeded the average. Small projects are generally shorter in duration and the opportunity to influence productivity levels is not as significant. The largest project suffers from being more complex and could not realize some of the same opportunities for gains in productivity.

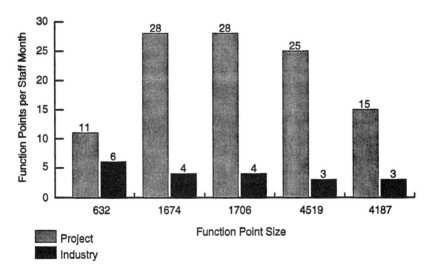

FIGURE 11.4 Comparison of Sapiens Project Rates to Industry Projections

In addition to the quantitative data analysis, a qualitative data analysis was also conducted. The results provided insights into some of the underlying reasons for the success of these projects. Certainly the Sapiens product and methodology contributed greatly to the positive results. Other contributing factors centered around high skill levels and the simple nature of these systems.

These projects were highly visible and were, therefore, treated somewhat differently from the mainstream. Sapiens' personnel were also involved in these efforts and therefore accounted for higher levels of productivity. Furthermore, the small projects were less productive because team size was too large. The larger the team size the more complicated the management effort.

This experience provides two dramatic insights. The first, and most obvious, result is the dramatic effect tools and skills can have on increasing productivity levels. Secondly, and perhaps more subtly, is the impact that measurement can have on an organization and the decisions it makes. Recall the initial objective Sapiens had with regard to software metrics:

"Raising the level of awareness within the marketplace regarding the availability and potential use of software metrics that could be used to aid clients in the purchasing and implementing of software and related tools".

Information is a powerful tool.

CHAPTER

12

OPPORTUNITY FOR AUTOMATION

INTRODUCTION

Function Point practitioners are commonly software developers; therefore, their natural orientation is toward automation. When discussing Function Points, sooner or later the question is raised regarding the availability of tools to automate the Function Point counting process and other software measurement practices. Currently, automation of software measurement is in its infancy. There is clearly a need to provide increased levels of automated functionality in support of measurement activities.

In this chapter we will introduce one possible approach for simple software measurement automation. This approach does not represent a futuristic multimedia plan for automation; it is simply a get started scenario that would be plausible given the current state of measurement techniques and related tools. The vision we have created is an automated solution that utilizes currently available tools and links them together in a strategy of total automation.

Discussing the topic of software measurement automation is perhaps a little misleading. It would be better described as measurement data collection and reporting automation. There are few tools available that automate the measurement process itself. For example, there are *no* tools currently available that automate the accurate counting of Function Points. There are tools available that effectively utilize entered Function Point data along with other measured influencers to predict fairly accurate estimates.

As an aid to those interested in pursuing automated support, we have developed a list (see Vendor Listing in Appendix F) of software providers and their tool offerings. It is only a partial list and should be used as a starting point. It is also focused on tools that relate to supporting the Function Point methodology. It would be far too involved to list all the tools and all the vendors that have software products that lay claim to supporting software measurement. We chose those vendors with which we are familiar or have observed at client sites and which appear to have been well received. Furthermore, an inclusive list of vendors might be a bit overwhelming and, therefore, ignored. We simply want to present you with a starting point. More comprehensive listings are available; the IFPUG office in Westerville, Ohio can supply you with a detailed list.

As a value added benefit, automation makes measurement data more accessible and broadens the audience that can share in the use of the data. If data is on-line and readily accessible, then there is the opportunity to share data across the street and around the world. We will close this chapter with a discussion about industry trends relative to on-line data availability.

SUPPORTING MEASUREMENT WITH AUTOMATION

The automation of an organization's software measurement process should be spirited by the need to enhance the rigor and the accuracy of accepted software measurement practices. Ideally, the approach to automation is similar to that of building a software system. You must develop a strategic plan that clearly states the need for measurement, the timeframe to implement the tools that will automate the process, and the cost of the tools. The goal should be nothing short of total automation. Total, in this context, means completing the measurement cycle. It does not refer to having every measurement process automated. Total automation will complete the loop from initial sizing to developing baseline data which will be available for future estimating.

Similar to the toolsets available to automate the development environment, measurement automation can be enhanced by tying together a variety of tools to form a measurement suite. Hopefully, one day in the not too distant future, we will see the commercial development of such a suite of tools. Software vendors such as Applied Business Technology and DDB Software are working toward that goal.

What we are automating are the management practices that measure and monitor the software development lifecycle. Four distinct phases of project management will be presented in our example: project planning, project tracking, project reporting, and baselining. In each of these phases we will present the opportunity for automation.

Project Planning

The first phase that we will automate is project planning (Figure 12.1). As we begin the development process, we must produce an estimate based upon a user request. Using the estimating model we discussed in Chapter 10, we know that we must consider size, complexity, and influencing factors. Therefore, the estimating process will size and assess the complexity of the user request using Function Point analysis. It will also make use of the data collected in our baseline to evaluate the impact of the various influencers. The result is a project estimate for schedule, effort, and cost. These results are stored in a repository and passed to the next phase of our project management model. Automated tools available include Function Point repositories for storing manually derived Function Point counts and partially automated counters that are driven by front-end design tools. The estimating process also is an opportunity for automation.

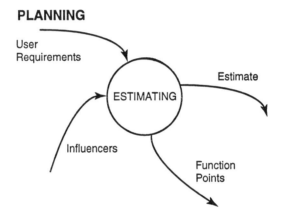

FIGURE 12.1   Project Estimating during the Planning Phase

Project Tracking

Once the work product has been agreed upon and properly estimated, the next step in the process is to track project activities during the design, build, and test phase (Figure 12.2). Project Tracking occurs throughout the development lifecycle and includes such things as time reporting, defect tracking, and managing changes in requirements scope. In our automated system, project time is recorded on a weekly basis and is input to a project scheduling and time reporting tool. The time data is also passed to our measurement repository to enable us to later compare plan to actual.

Formal reviews and inspections are conducted at each major milestone. As defects are found they are recorded and entered into the defect tracking system. The defect tracking system keeps up-to-date records on which defects have been cor-

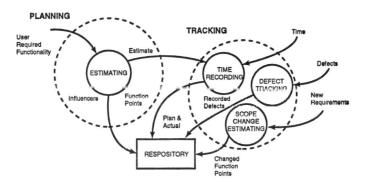

FIGURE 12.2   Tracking and Storing Project Actuals

rected. It also analyzes the development process based on additional information that is captured during the review and inspection process. The origin, severity, and type of defect is collected. The system will automatically assess the effectiveness of the development process by analyzing the origin of the defects. The point of discovery may not be where the defect originated. Defect data is passed to the repository. As changes in scope are introduced we naturally will need to develop new estimates. These estimates are calculated, and changes in scope, estimated delivery dates, and costs are tracked through the repository.

Project Reporting

At any time during our project management activities, or at the completion of the project, we can assess our progress through the use of an automated Management Information System tool for executive reporting. This component of our automated system provides data to a variety of audiences including project managers, development supervisors, and senior level executives. Each reporting level can readily obtain the data it needs to monitor and manage the software development process. Organizational performance data, project profiles and application assessments can all be accessed by this function (Figure 12.3).

Project Baselining

The final stage of our automation environment is baselining (Figure 12.4). As you recall from Chapter 2, baselining involves the bringing together of quantitative and qualitative data to yield performance profiles. It incorporates the collecting, analyzing, and directing of data to manage the software development processes. As data is collected on a project by project basis, that information populates the central repository and contributes to the baseline. Another possible method of baseline development requires an intensified effort to collect data from a variety of recently com-

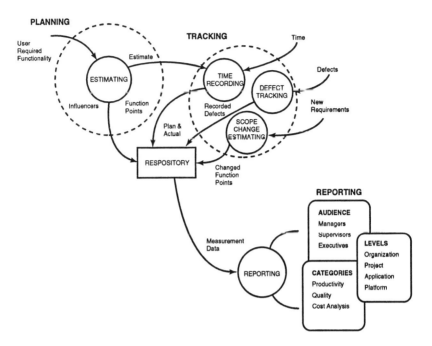

FIGURE 12.3   Reporting Key Measurement Data to the Organization

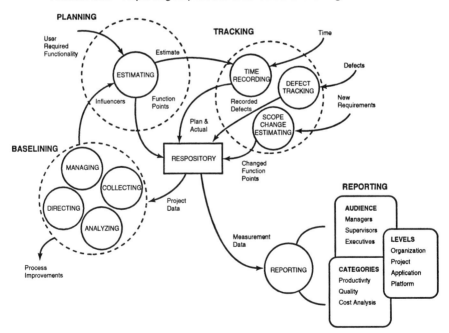

FIGURE 12.4   Building a Baseline of Historical Project Data

pleted projects. This process is used in instances where an organization may require a jump start to their measurement program or require immediate performance data.

Once the baseline data collection and reporting process has begun, the value of the possible deliverables is tremendous. Project and organization profiles depict performance levels based on a number of variables. Highly productive projects can be compared to the lower yielding projects for an assessment of software process strengths and weaknesses. At an organizational level these same characteristics may be examined with the results indicating improvement opportunities required across the organization.

We have chosen to take a simple look at the opportunities for automation and to present what may be considered simply a good starting place. Measurement does not have to be burdensome. Through the automation of measurement practices, productivity and accuracy improvements can be realized in the data collection and reporting process.

Let's consider for a moment the impact that accurate counting and capturing of Function Point data might have on an organization. Studies show that when a rigorous and consistent counting practice is lacking, Function Point counts could vary by 10% or more. If an organization is counting 10,000 Function Points a year we might see a swing of 1000 Function Points. If you use industry cost per Function Point averages, a 10% variance would come to a whopping $1,000,000. That could be a significant variance if you are using this data to plan a budget, chargeback expenses, or allocate resources. Automating the software measurement practice is not going to result in perfectly accurate data, but it will provide consistency and rigor to the process and will allow a greater opportunity for increased accuracy.

INDUSTRY DATA: ON-LINE ALL THE TIME

Earlier we suggested that software measurement automation has the potential to make data more accessible, and we made reference of linkages to industry data. Currently, industry software measurement data is outdated, inaccessible, and is so generalized as to be of little value to the consumer. What we need instead is current data reflecting current trends. We need data that is accessible by the consumer.

As we move towards the automated collection, storage, and reporting of measurement data we will see measurement data warehouses being developed. These warehouses will have stores of industry data that can be made available to the consumer. Ultimately, this data will become available over the Internet. On a subscription fee basis, clients will contribute data and access data from these data stores. Each storage area of data may represent a vertical market segment. Perhaps, all industry data will be housed in one larger centralized repository.

Now imagine that our suite of tools is linked into that repository. You would have access to your data base of knowledge and a window into the entire world of measurements data. When you want to know the impact of a new tool or method on your environment, you can call upon this data to conduct your what-if analysis. This is not a wide-eyed dream. As of the writing of this book, both authors were preparing talks on this subject matter.

APPENDIX

HINTS TO HELP WITH COUNTING

HINTS TO HELP WITH COUNTING ILFS AND EIFS

The following hints from the *Counting Practice Manual* may help you apply the ILF and EIF counting rules. (**Caution:** These hints are not rules and should not be used as rules.)

1. Is the data a logical group that fulfills specific user requirements?
    - ↪ An application can use an ILF or EIF in multiple processes, but the ILF or EIF is counted only once.
    - ↪ Do not assume that one physical file equals one logical file when viewing data logically from the user perspective.
    - ↪ Although some storage technologies such as tables in a relational DBMS or a sequential flat file relate closely to ILFs or EIFs, do not assume that this always equals a one-to-one, physical-logical relationship.
    - ↪ If a group of data was not counted as an ILF or EIF itself, count its data elements as DETs for the ILF or EIF which includes that group of data.

    ↪ Do not assume all physical files must be counted or included as part of an ILF or EIF.

2. Where is data maintained? Inside or outside the application boundary?

    ↪ Look at the work flow.

    ↪ In the process functional decomposition, identify where the user and other application interfaces occur.

    ↪ Work through the process diagram to get hints.

    ↪ Credit ILFs maintained by more than one application to each application at the time the application is counted.

3. Is the data in an ILF maintained through an elementary process of the application?

    ↪ An application can use an ILF or EIF multiple times, but you count the ILF or EIF only once.

    ↪ Work through the process diagram to get hints.

    ↪ Credit ILFs maintained by more than one application to each application at the time the application is counted.

Hints to Help with Counting EIs

The following hints from the *Counting Practice Manual* may help you apply the EI counting rules. (**Caution:** The hints are not rules and should not be used as rules.)

1. Is data received from outside the application boundary?

    ↪ Look at the work flow.

    ↪ Identify where the user and other application interfaces occur in the process functional decomposition.

2. Is the process the smallest unit of activity from the user perspective?

    ↪ Look at the different forms used.

    ↪ Review the ILFs to identify how the user groups the information.

    ↪ Identify where the user and other application interfaces occur in the process functional decomposition.

    ↪ Look at what happened in the manual system.

    ↪ Note that one physical input or transaction file or screen can, when viewed logically, correspond to one EI if the processing logic is identical.

3. Is the process self-contained and does it leave the business in a consistent state?

    ↪ Review external outputs and external inquiries to understand how the user works with the information.

    ↪ Work through the process diagram to get hints.

    ↪ Look at what happened in the manual system.

⇀ Check for consistency with other decisions.

4. Is the processing logic unique from other EIs?

⇀ Identify batch inputs based on the processing logic required.

5. Are the data elements different from those for other EIs?

⇀ If the data elements appear to be a subset for the data elements of another external input, be sure two elementary processes are required by the user, one for the main data elements and one for the subsets.

Hints to Help with Counting EOs

The following hints from the *Counting Practice Manual* may help you apply the EO counting rules. (**Caution:** The hints are not rules and should not be used as rules.)

1. Is data sent outside the application boundary?

⇀ Look at the work flow.

⇀ Identify where the user and other application interfaces occur in the process functional decomposition.

2. Is the process the smallest unit of activity from the user perspective?

⇀ Look at the different forms used.

⇀ Review the ILFs to identify how the user groups the information.

⇀ Identify where the user and other application interfaces occur in the process functional decomposition.

⇀ Look at what happened in the manual system.

⇀ Remember that one physical report, screen, or batch output file can, when viewed logically, correspond to a number of EOs.

⇀ Remember that two or more physical reports, screens, or batch output files can correspond to one EO if the processing logic is identical.

3. Is the process self-contained and does it leave the business in a consistent state?

⇀ Review external inputs and external inquiries to get an overall view of how the user works with the information.

⇀ Work through the process diagram to get hints.

⇀ Look at what happened in the manual system.

⇀ Check for consistency with other decisions.

4. Is the processing logic unique from the other EOs?

⇀ Identify batch output based on the processing logic required.

⇀ Remember that resorting or rearranging a set of data does not make processing logic unique.

5. Are the data elements different from those for other EOs?

⇀ If the data elements appear to be a subset for the data elements of another

EO, be sure two elementary processes are required by the user, one for the main data elements and one for the subsets.

Hints to Help with Counting EQs

The following hints from the *Counting Practice Manual* may help you apply the EQ counting rules. (**Caution:** The hints are not rules and should not be used as rules.)

1. Is data directly retrieved from an ILF or EIF?
   - ⇌ Look at the work flow.
   - ⇌ Identify where the user and other application interfaces occur in the process functional decomposition.
2. Is the process the smallest unit of activity from the user perspective?
   - ⇌ Review the ILFs to identify how the user groups the information.
   - ⇌ Identify where the user and other application interfaces occur in the process functional decomposition.
   - ⇌ Look at what happened in the manual system.
   - ⇌ Remember that one physical report or screen can, when viewed logically, correspond to a number of EQs.
   - ⇌ Remember that two physical reports or screens can correspond to one EQ if the processing logic is identical.
3. Is the process self-contained and does it leave the business in a consistent state?
   - ⇌ Review external inputs and external outputs to get an overall view of how the user works with the information.
   - ⇌ Work through the process diagram to get hints.
4. Is the processing logic unique from other EQs?
   - ⇌ Look for derived data to distinguish inquiries from outputs.
   - ⇌ Remember that resorting or rearranging a set of data does not make processing logic unique.
5. Are the data elements different from those for other EQs?
   - ⇌ If the data elements appear to be a subset for the data elements of another external inquiry, be sure two elementary processes are required by the user, one for the main data elements and one for the subsets.

WHO SHOULD COUNT

Knowledge of the project/application and of Function Point counting is required:

1. Application Knowledge is required to understand the user requirements.

- Customers
- Marketing personnel
- Functional experts
- Development/Maintenance team members

2. Function Point Knowledge is required to size those user requirements.
- Measurement analysts
- Function Point specialists
- Knowledgeable personnel in application/project

Involvement in your organization is dependent upon your methodology to implement Function Points, your organizational structure, and the types of projects and applications being developed.

USEFUL PROJECT/APPLICATION DOCUMENTATION

The following documents are useful in identifying the functionality which exists in a project or an application:

- High level system diagrams (relationships to other interacting applications)
- Logical data models/process models
- Entity relationship models
- Design specifications
- Requirements
- Functional specifications
- Systems specifications
- Detail design specifications
- Layouts of files and databases
- On-line screen prints
- Report layouts
- Messages
- User manuals
- Customer training materials

FUNCTION POINT COUNTING DOCUMENTATION

The following are useful in identifying function types and in providing rules to accomplish a Function Point Count:

Previous Function Point Analysis

- ↝ Application boundary definitions
- ↝ Past Function Point counts

Function Point Counting Guidelines

- ↝ IFPUG Manual
- ↝ Local counting guidelines
- ↝ Counting/analysis worksheets
- ↝ Quick reference cards
- ↝ Counting matrices

FUNCTION POINT WORKSHEETS

FUNCTION POINT COUNT SUMMARY

Project Number _____   **Project Name** _____
Date of Count _____   **Counter's Name** _____

Instructions: Enter all function types included. For development and initial
Function Point counts there will not be any entries in the Before columns. Annotate all function types added by the conversion. You may wish to use different sheets for files and transactions.

Description	Type	DETs	RETs/FTRs	Complexity	DETs	RETs/FTRs	Complexity
	ILF/EIF EI/EO/EQ	After	After	After	Before	Before	Before

FUNCTION POINT CALCULATION TABLE

Project Number _____ Project Name _____

Type of Count: Development Project / Application Count (circle one)

Phase of Count: Proposal/Requirements/Design/Code/Test /
Delivery (circle one)

Date of Count _____ Counter's Name _____

*Function Types	Low	Average	High	Total
External Inputs	×3	×4	×6	
External Outputs	×4	×5	×7	
External Inquiries	×3	×4	×6	
Internal Logical Files	×7	×10	×15	
External Interface Files	×5	×7	×10	

Total Unadjusted Function Points (UFPs) =

GENERAL SYSTEMS CHARACTERISTICS

Characteristic	Degree of Influence	Characteristic	Degree of Influence
1. Data Communication	_____	8. On-line Update	_____
2. Distributed Functions	_____	9. Complex Processing	_____
3. Performance	_____	10. Reusability	_____
4. Heavily Used Configuration	_____	11. Installation Ease	_____
5. Transaction Rate	_____	12. Operational Ease	_____
6. On-line Data Entry	_____	13. Multiple Site	_____
7. End User Efficiency	_____	14. Facilitate Change	_____

Total Degree of Influence =

Value Adjustment Factor (VAF) = .65 + (.01 × TDI) = _____

Final Function Point Count (FP) = UFP × VAF = _____

*Development Function Point Count includes function types added by the conversion. Application Function Point Count does not include conversion requirements. An application count after an enhancement must include all existing function types, including those unchanged.

FUNCTION POINT CALCULATION TABLE

Project Number _____   Project Name _____

Type of Count: Enhancement Project Count

Phase of Count: Proposal/Requirements/Design/Code/Test /
Delivery (circle one)

Date of Count _____   Counter's Name _____

---

*Function Types (Value After)	Low	Average	High	Total
External Inputs	×3	×4	×6	
External Outputs	×4	×5	×7	
External Inquiries	×3	×4	×6	
Internal Logical Files	×7	×10	×15	
External Interface Files	×5	×7	×10	

Unadjusted After Function Points = _____

Enhancement Function Point Count includes function types added by the conversion.

**Function Types Deleted	Low	Average	High	Total
External Inputs	×3	×4	×6	
External Outputs	×4	×5	×7	
External Inquiries	×3	×4	×6	
Internal Logical Files	×7	×10	×15	
External Interface Files	×5	×7	×10	

Unadjusted Deleted Function Points = _____

(continued on page 181)

*Include added function types and modified function types (value after).
**Includes those function types deleted by the Enhancement.

FUNCTION POINT CALCULATION TABLE

Project Number _____ Project Name _____

GENERAL SYSTEMS CHARACTERISTICS

Characteristic	Degree of Influence		Characteristic	Degree of Influence	
	Before	**After**		**Before**	**After**
1. Data Communication	___	___	8. On-line Update	___	___
2. Distributed Functions	___	___	9. Complex		
3. Performance	___	___	Processing	___	___
4. Heavily Used			10. Reusability	___	___
Configuration	___	___	11. Installation Ease	___	___
5. Transaction Rate	___	___	12. Operational Ease	___	___
6. On-line Data Entry	___	___	13. Multiple Site	___	___
7. End User Efficiency	___	___	14. Facilitate Change	___	___

Total Degree of Influence =

Value Adjustment Factor Before (VAFB) = .65 + (.01 × TDI Before) = _____

Value Adjustment Factor After (VAFA) = .65 + (.01 × TDI After) = _____

Enhancement Project Function Point Count:
(Function Types (After) × VAFA) + (Function Types Deleted × VAFB) = _____

C

PRACTICE FUNCTION POINT SPECIALIST CERTIFICATION EXAM

The International Function Point Users Group (IFPUG) Certification Committee provides certification of Function Point Counters, training materials, and tools. You can determine who has been certified by calling the IFPUG office in Westerville, Ohio at (614) 895–7130.

Counters are certified by passing a Certified Function Point Specialist (CFPS) examination. We have provided a similar exam, so you can determine, on your own, how well prepared you are to take the CFPS examination. Our practice exam follows in three parts. You should be able to complete the exam within three hours. Good luck.

PART I

1. The objectives of Function Point counting are to:
   a. Measure what the user requested and received
   b. Measure independently of technology used for implementation
   c. Provide a vehicle for software estimation
   d. All of the above

2. An application function point count:
   a. Is also referred to as the Baseline or Installed Function Point Count
   b. Includes the functionality provided by data conversion and associated conversion reporting requirements
   c. Is altered every time an enhancement alters the application's function
   d. a and c

3. Internal logical files are:
   a Stored external to the application's boundary
   b. Maintained through a standardized process of the application
   c. Identified as a requirement of the application by the users
   d. b and c

4. An external interface file (EIF) can be:
   a. A user identifiable group of logically related data, utilized by the application, but mainitained by another application
   b. A user identifiable group of logically related control information, maintained by the application
   c. A user identifiable group of logically related data maintained by the application but which is referenced only in another part of the application
   d. a and b

5. An external input is considered unique if:
   a. Data is maintained on one or more internal logical file(s)
   b. The input data fields are unique
   c. The processing logic is unique
   d. All of the above

6. External outputs can include:
   a. Data sent external to the application's boundary
   b. Control information sent external to the application's boundary
   c. Help text returned to the user
   d. a and b

7. The following can be external inquiries:
   a. Help text
   b. Menu screens that provide only navigation
   c. Derived data
   d. System documentation that is available on-line, in lieu of or in addition to that available in hard copy

8. Examples of General System Characteristics do not include:
   a. Installation ease
   b. Language
   c. End user efficiency
   d. Data communication

9. Flexible query/report capability is accounted for in which of the following GSCs?

    a. Installation ease

    b. Facilitate change

    c. Performance

    d. End user efficiency

10. Which of the following should be counted as a DET on an EI?

    a. Command line(s) or PF/Action key(s) that provide the capability to specify the action to be taken by the external input

    b. Error messages as a result of the EI transaction

    c. Fields relating to the EI transaction

    d. All of the above

11. Help within an application includes Full Screen Help, Field Sensitive Help, and System Help. How many EQs are counted?

    a. One for each screen

    b. Two for each screen

    c. Three for the application

    d. None of the above

12. TDI is:

    a. The sum of the 14 Degrees of Influence

    b. The Value Adjustment Factor

    c. +/− 35%

    d. None of the above

13. Classify, as high complexity, internal logical files or external interface files which:

    a. Contain more than 50 DETs and 2 RETs

    b. Contain more than 5 RETs

    c. Contain more than 100 DETs

    d. a and c

14. An application's specific user functionality is evaluated in terms of:

    a. What is delivered by the application

    b. How it is delivered by the application

    c. Which user requested and visible components are counted

    d. a and c

15. Boundaries:

    a. Identify the border between the application or project being measured and either external applications or the user domain

    b. Establish the scope of the work product being measured

    c. Consider the application from the user's point of view, what the user can understand and describe

    d. All of the above

16. Which of the following can equate to one or more ILFs?

    a. Application data

    b. Application security data

   c. Error messages

   d. All of the above

17. Which of the following can equate to one or more EIFs?

   a. Reference data utilized by the application, but not maintained

   b. Help messages

   c. Error messages

   d. All of the above

18. Unique processing logic for EIs includes:

   a. Edits

   b. Calculations

   c. Algorithms

   d. All of the above

19. Which of the following are external outputs?

   a. Data residing on an ILF which is formatted and processed for use by an external application

   b. Error/confirmation messages associated with EIs

   c. Error/confirmation messages associated with EQs

   d. All of the above

20. Which of the following can not be counted as external inquiries:

   a. Selection of data retrieval based on data input

   b. Data retrieval capabilities prior to change/delete functionality provided the inquiry capability can be and is used as a stand alone function

   c. Log-on screens without security

   d. Full screen Help

21. Degrees of Influence (DI) are evaluated:

   a. On a scale of zero to five

   b. For each transaction

   c. On a scale of +/− 35%

   d. All of the above

22. Security or timing considerations are accounted for in which of the following GSCs?

   a. Distributed data processing

   b. Heavily used configuration

   c. End user efficiency

   d. On-line data entry

23. Which of the following fields on an internal logical file are counted as multiple DETs?

   a. An account number or date that is physically stored in multiple fields

   b. Fields that appear more than once in an internal logical file because of technology or implementation techniques

   c. Summary fields at the monthly, quarterly, and annual level

    d. Repeating fields that are identical in format and exist to allow for multiple occurrences of a data value

24. When applied, the Value Adjustment Factor adjusts the Unadjusted Function Point Count:
    a. +/– 5%
    b. +/– 35%
    c. 65%
    d. None of the above

25. Which of the following is not an EI?
    a. Unique external data used to maintain an ILF
    b. A physical input file
    c. Each unique batch process which maintains an ILF
    d. Each unique screen function that maintains an ILF

26. A File Type Referenced (FTR) is counted for:
    a. Each internal logical file maintained or referenced during the processing of an external input
    b. Each external interface file referenced during the processing of an external input
    c. a and b
    d. None of the above

27. A development function point count:
    a. Is associated with the initial installation of new software
    b. Measures the function provided to the end users by the project
    c. Includes the functionality provided by data conversion and associated conversion reporting requirements
    d. All of the above

28. Which of the following can equate to one or more ILFs?
    a. Work files
    b. Edit data
    c. Sort files
    d. All of the above

29. Which of the following can equate to one or more EIFs?
    a. Data received from another application that adds, changes, or deletes data on an ILF
    b. Edit data used by the application to validate inputs
    c. Data maintained by the application being counted, but accessed and utilized by another application
    d. Data formatted and processed for use by another application

30. Which of the following is an incorrect statement?
    a. An EI processes data or processes control information which enters the application's external boundary
    b. Control information must directly maintain an internal logical file
    c. Control information is data used by a process within an application

boundary to assure compliance with business function requirements specified by the user

d. Processed data must maintain an internal logical file

31. Multiple External Outputs are counted for:
    a. Identical reports which have the same format and processing logic, but exist due to unique data values
    b. Summary fields on a detail report
    c. Two identically formatted reports at the detail and summary levels
    d. The creation (through the use of a language such as FOCUS or SQL) of an undefined number of reports

32. An external inquiry (EQ) is:
    a. A unique input/output combination that results in the retrieval of data
    b. Does not contain derived data
    c. Does not update an internal logical file
    d. All of the above

33. Multilingual support counts as how many items under end user efficiency?
    a. None
    b. Six
    c. Two
    d. One

34. Which of the following are counted as DETs on EOs?
    a. Each user recognizable, non-recursive field that appears on the external output
    b. Each unique command/parameter in a report generator facility requested by the user for do-it-yourself report generation
    c. Each type of label and each type of numberical equivalent in a graphical output
    d. All of the above

35. The Unadjusted Function Point Count is:
    a. The sum of the weighted function type values of the application being measured
    b. Multiplied by the Value Adjustment Factor to arrive at the Adjusted Function Point Count
    c. The general application processing complexities based on 14 General System Characteristics
    d. a and b

36. An enhancement function point count:
    a. Measures the modifications to the existing application that add, change, or delete user function within the scope of a project
    b. Does not include the functionality provided by data conversion and associated conversion reporting requirements
    c. Represents the count of the installed application when completed
    d. All of the above

37. Back-up files are counted as ILFs if:
    a. Specifically requested by the user to meet legal or similar requirements
    b. Required for normal back-up and recovery procedures
    c. Introduced only because of technology used
    d. a and b

38. Which of the following are EIs?
    a. External reference data utilized by the application, but not maintained on internal logical files
    b. Data input used to drive selection for data retrieval
    c. User updates to a Help file
    d. Log-on screens with security

39. An EI can be invoked by entering "A" or "Add" on a command line or by using a PF key. How many EIs should be counted?
    a. Zero
    b. One
    c. Two
    d. Three

40. If a report generator facilty is requested by the user as part of an application for do-it-yourself report generation, the functionality is recognized by which of the following GSCs?
    a. Heavily used configuration
    b. Complex processing
    c. Installation ease
    d. Facilitate change

41. Which of the following could be counted as multiple EQs?
    a. Identical queries, produced on different media due to specific user requirements
    b. Different graphical displays requested by the user
    c. Multiple methods of invoking the same inquiry logic
    d. a and b

42. Extensive logical processing is accounted for in which of the following GSCs?
    a. Transaction rate
    b. On-line data entry
    c. Complex processing
    d. Performance

43. Which of the following are counted as DETs on EOs?
    a. Literals on reports
    b. Paging variables or system generated time/date stamps
    c. Each distinct error or confirmation message available for display on an external input
    d. None of the above

44. An average complexity EIF has an Unadjusted Function Point value of:
   a. 5
   b. 7
   c. 10
   d. 15

45. To assign an Unadjusted Function Point value to each External Inquiry:
   a. Calculate the functional complexity based on the input side of the external inquiry
   b. Calcualte the functional complexity based on the output side of the external inquiry
   c. Select the higher of the two functional complexities, based on both the input side and the output side
   d. None of the above

PART II

1. The Unadjusted Function Point value of an ILF with 21 DETs and 3 RETs is:
   a. 5
   b. 7
   c. 10
   d. 15

2. The Unadjusted Function Point value for a project which includes 3 low complexity EIs, 1 low complexity EO, 1 average complexity EQ, and 1 low complexity ILF is:
   a. 23
   b. 24
   c. 25
   d. 27

3. How many EIs are counted on a screen which permits a user to add a customer, view customer information, delete a customer, and change customer information?
   a. One
   b. Two
   c. Three
   d. Four

4. An enhancement is planned for application A. An EI is being revised from 12 DETs and 1 FTR by adding a DET and an FTR. The EI will now have 13 DETs and 2 FTRs. The unadjusted value of this EI towards the Enhancement Function Point Count is:
   a. 3
   b. 4

c. 6

d. None of the above

5. The increase in the value of the Application Unadjusted Function Point Count for the question 4 above is:

a. 1

b. 4

c. 3

d. 6

6. The Accounts Payable (AP) Application sends a transaction to the General Ledger (GL) Application which updates an ILF in GL. How is the transaction counted?

a. As an EIF to AP and an EI to GL

b. As an EO to AP and EIF to GL

c. As both an EIF and an EI to GL

d. As an EO to AP and an EI to GL

7. The Payroll Application provides the capability to the user to extract information maintained in three separate ILFs. The user enters an ID # and a function key. One screen display is provided in response with ten retrieved fields. There is no derived information. What is counted?

a. A low EI, an average EO, and a high EQ

b. A high EQ

c. A low EQ

d. An average EQ

8. A report generator facility for the do-it-yourselfer provides twelve different selction parameters for reports. The file is not saved. What is counted?

a. 12 EIs, 12 EOs, and 1 ILF

b. 12 EOs and 1 ILF

c. 12 EIs and 12 EOs

d. 12 EIs and 1 EO

9. A screen provides capability for the user to add the following data to an ILF: Employee ID, Employee Name, Employee Job Title, Employee Job Location, and Employee Phone Number using one of three possible keys: A, Add, or <ENTER>. How many DETs are counted in the EI?

a. 1

b. 6

c. 7

d. 8

10. An External Output can be displayed in tabular form, as a pie chart or as a bar chart. How many EOs are counted?

a. 1

b. 2 (one for table, one for graphics)

c. 3

d. None of the above

11. An ILF is updated by three separate applications (A, B, and C). Where is it counted?
    a. In the largest application
    b. In the application where it experiences the most use
    c. In all three applications
    d. In the application where most of the data is maintained

12. Security requirements of an application require a user to enter a password to gain access to that application. How is the password entry requirement counted?
    a. As an EI
    b. As an EO
    c. As an EQ
    d. Not counted

13. What is the Project Unadjusted Function Point Count for an enhancement which includes the following: one new high EI, one new average EO, and one ILF revised from low to average?
    a. 21
    b. 16
    c. 18
    d. 23

14. Data is collected upon entry into a temporary file. The temporary file is sorted before being loaded to an employee file. The employee file is maintained and utilized to create reports. How many ILFs are counted?
    a. 0
    b. 1
    c. 2
    d. 3

15. Three user defined groups of data are combined into one flat file. How many ILFs are counted?
    a. 0
    b. 1
    c. 2
    d. 3

16. One user defined customer file is developed by providing three data based tables: customer, address, and point of contact. How many ILFs are counted?
    a. 0
    b. 1
    c. 2
    d. 3

17. Users have requested the use of three screens to accomplish one update transaction. How is it counted?
    a. One EI
    b. Three EIs

    c. One EI and two EQs

    d. None of the above

18. Which of the following can not be ILFs?

    a. Application data

    b. Error messages maintained by users

    c. JCL

    d. Help messages maintained by users

19. An ILF:

    a. Is only read within the boundary of the application being counted

    b. Is maintained by the application being counted

    c. May contain control information

    d. b and c

20. Application A maintains an ILF that is also read by Application B. Application A should:

    a. Get credit for an ILF and an EIF

    b. Get credit for an ILF

    c. Get credit for an EO

    d. b and c

21. Examples of EIs include:

    a. Batch input that adds data to an ILF

    b. Batch input that initiates a search for data to be printed

    c. Batch data that is referenced from another application

    d. Header records on a batch file of transactions

22. An application utilizes two media in updating an ILF with exactly the same information. One input is keyed. The other input takes place by scanning a bar code:

    a. Count both input types if they are specifically requested by the user

    b. Never count duplicate inputs if the same data is updated

    c. Media is not considered in function point counting

    d. a and b

23. When counting DETs in an EO:

    a. Literals in the heading should always be counted

    b. Dates in the heading that are system generated should not be counted

    c. Any information in headings should be counted

    d. a and b

24. The functional complexity of EOs is determined by:

    a. The number of DETs and the number of RETs

    b. The number of FTRs and the number of RETs

    c. The number of DETs and the number of FTRs

    d. a and c

25. External inquiries:

    a. Always have an input side and an output side

b. Sometimes have derived fields on the output side

c. Can have a printed reponse

d. a and c

26. Which of the following cannot be EQs?
   a. Navigation
   b. Log on screens with security
   c. Screen displays that contain derived data
   d. a and c

27. The possible range of adjustment to an unadjusted function point count based on the General Systems Characteristics is:
   a. +/– 35%
   b. 0 to 5
   c. 35%
   d. None of the above

28. Which of the following is not an EO?
   a. An error message associated with an EI on-line
   b. An error message associated with an EQ on-line
   c. On-line derived report requested via report selection menu
   d. a and b

29. Which is not an example of an EQ?
   a. Field sensitive help
   b. Log-on screens that have no security
   c. Selection menu screens with no retrieved data
   d. b and c

30. When determining the Value Adjustment Factor for an enhancement project:
   a. Use the Value Adjustment Factor from the previous project
   b. Value Adjustment Factor is not used
   c. Evaluate and include the influence of the questions as they apply to a project
   d. Evaluate and include the influence of the questions as they apply to a project within an application boundary after completion of the project

31. When determining the Value Adjustment Factor:
   a. Select and total scores for all statements within each characteristic that apply to an application
   b. Select the statement for each characteristic that most clearly describes the application
   c. Include the scores for all fourteen characteristics when determining the Value Adjustment Factor
   d. b and c

32. Application A has a master file, Parts, that contains parts inventory information. Application B uses Parts as an external interface file. Application A counts Parts as:

    a. ILF and EIF
    b. ILF only
    c. EIF only
    d. None of the above

33. The Marketing System reports sales in detail for the branch managers and, using the same format, summary totals for the marketing director. How many external outputs are there?
    a. One, the sales report
    b. Two, sales report detail for the branch manager and sales report summary for the marketing director
    c. One for each of the branch managers and one for the marketing director
    d. None of the above

34. The Sales System sends a file of completed orders to the Billing System. The Sales System counts this file of orders as an:
    a. External interface file
    b. External output
    c. Internal logical file
    d. None of the above

35. The Branch Manager Sales Report is issued on paper and on microfiche as requested by the user. How many external outputs are there?
    a. One, the sales report
    b. Two, paper sales report and microfiche sales report
    c. Three, paper and microfiche sales reports plus the report file
    d. None of the above

36. System A has four menus of selection functionality for navigation through the system. How many external inquiries should be counted?
    a. One
    b. Four
    c. None
    d. One for each potential selection

37. The maximum Total Degree of Influence is:
    a. 35
    b. 65
    c. 70
    d. 135

38. My Unadjusted Function Points total 100. The total of my fourteen General System Characteristics is 35. What is my Adjusted Function Point count?
    a. 100
    b. 135
    c. 114
    d. None of the above

39. The original Unadjusted Function Points for an application were 400 with a

Value Adjustment Factor of 1.10. The first enhancement adds 30 function points and deletes 10. The functions being changed were originally worth 12 function points and are now worth 15. The Value Adjustment Factor will stay the same. What is the size of the enhancement project?

a. 57.2
b. 60.5
c. 55
d. 47.3

40. The original unadjusted function points for an application were 400 with a Value Adjustment Factor of 1.10. The first enhancement adds 30 function points and deletes 10. The functions being changed were originally worth 12 function points are now worth 15. The Value Adjustment Factor will stay the same. What is the size of the application after the enhancement?

a. 478.5
b. 465.3
c. 462
d. 463

41. An ILF consisting of 250 DETs has five RETs with 20, 110, 60, 50, and 10 DETs. The file should be counted as:

a. One high complexity ILF
b. Two high complexity ILFs and three low complexity ILFs
c. Two average complexity ILFs and three low complexity ILFs
d. Three average complexity ILFs and two low complexity ILFs

42. An EI has 16 DETs and 2 FTRs. What is its Unadjusted Function Point value?

a. 6
b. 5
c. 4
d. 3

43. An EO has 16 DETs and 3 FTRs. What is its Unadjusted Function Point value?

a. 7
b. 6
c. 5
d. 4

44. An ILF has 50 DETs and 1 RET. What is its Unadjusted Function Point value?

a. 5
b. 7
c. 10
d. 15

45. An EIF has 20 DETs and 2 RETs. What is its Unadjusted Function Point value?

a. 5
b. 7
c. 10
d. 15

PART III

Three problems follow (A, B, and C). Complete the appropriate answer sheets for each problem.

A. The David Consulting Group plans to build a simple locator application to maintain information about companies interested in their function point courses.

1. The logical grouping of **company contact data** to be maintained will include the following data fields:

company
name of contact
job title
initial contact (date)
street address
city
state
zip code
phone number
fax number

This data will initially be created when an individual indicates an interest in any course. Employees will have the capability for creating, changing, and deleting, via an on-line screen, the above information using the following commands: Add or A, Change or C, Delete or D.

2. Additional fields to be included in the **company contact data,** but updated with separate transactions, are as follows:

packet sent (date)
phone contact (date)

a. These fields are to be maintained by two separate functions as follows:

(1) When an information packet is sent, the individual mailing the package will use a separate screen to enter company, name of contact, and the date the packet was sent, using a function key.

(2) A phone follow-up should be made within two weeks of the mailing to ensure receipt and respond to questions. When this contact has been completed, the caller will use a separate screen to enter

company, name of contact, date of the contact, and notes, using a function key. The date of contact will be used to update the **company contact data**. The notes will update a logical grouping of **notes data**, which is maintained by another application.

b. The **notes data file** contains the following data fields:

company
name of contact
date of contact
notes (text)

Functionality within the locator application will permit only the addition and/or retrieval of notes to this file and only via this screen. Existing notes should be retrieved by striking a function key; only data from the **notes data file** will be displayed.

3. A menu driven system will be required to navigate through the system. The six functions offering selection will be as follows:

create company contact
retrieve company contact
update company contact
delete company contact
packet sent
phone contact/notes

a. All of these functions, except retrieve company contact, were discussed above. The retrieval will display only the fields maintained in the **company contact data.**

b. Errors will be returned from an externally maintained error file, which has only four fields. One of these fields contains the error messages. Errors will be returned for each of the above transactions; the maximum number of unique error messages for a transaction is eight.

4. Identify the functions included above and their complexities, using the answer sheet for Part III, Problem A.

B. For the exercise just completed, compute the Function Point Calculation Table using your functions and the data already entered on the table to compute a Final (Adjusted) Function Point Count. (Do not leave any spaces blank.) The table is provided as the answer sheet for Part III, Problem B.

C. Shortly after the locator application was delivered, Caren Garmus stated that she wanted to utilize the Help sub-system already being maintained by an external application to provide both field and screen level Help. These two levels of Help will be available on each screen and will access Help from two separately maintained external Help files (Field Help and Screen Help). Help, in all cases, has less than five fields.

1. Mary Herron said she wanted a weekly Overdue Contact Report which would indicate those contacts which had not received packets and those contacts who had not been called within two weeks of the mailing. The report would retrieve the data from the **company contact data file:**

   <u>Overdue Contact Report</u>   <u>Date Printed</u>   <u>Page #</u>
   Retrieval as of:
   Company:
   Name of Contact:
   Initial Contact Date:
   Packet Sent (blank if not sent; date if sent):
   Phone Contact Due Date (blank if no packet sent or 14 days after packet sent):

2. Identify the functions and their complexities for the Help and Overdue Contact Report functions. Additionally, for the report, identify the number of DETs and FTRs. It is not necessary to enter the number of DETs/RETs/FTRs for the Help functions. Use the answer sheet for Part III, Problem C.

CFPS PRACTICE EXAMINATION BLANK ANSWER SHEETS

ANSWER SHEET, PART I

Name: _____

Instructions: Darken your answer to each question. Only one answer is correct. Recommend use of pencil. To delete an answer, cross through with an X.

1. a	b	c	d	**16.** a	b	c	d	**31.** a	b	c	d
2. a	b	c	d	**17.** a	b	c	d	**32.** a	b	c	d
3. a	b	c	d	**18.** a	b	c	d	**33.** a	b	c	d
4. a	b	c	d	**19.** a	b	c	d	**34.** a	b	c	d
5. a	b	c	d	**20.** a	b	c	d	**35.** a	b	c	d
6. a	b	c	d	**21.** a	b	c	d	**36.** a	b	c	d
7. a	b	c	d	**22.** a	b	c	d	**37.** a	b	c	d
8. a	b	c	d	**23.** a	b	c	d	**38.** a	b	c	d
9. a	b	c	d	**24.** a	b	c	d	**39.** a	b	c	d
10. a	b	c	d	**25.** a	b	c	d	**40.** a	b	c	d
11. a	b	c	d	**26.** a	b	c	d	**41.** a	b	c	d
12. a	b	c	d	**27.** a	b	c	d	**42.** a	b	c	d
13. a	b	c	d	**28.** a	b	c	d	**43.** a	b	c	d
14. a	b	c	d	**29.** a	b	c	d	**44.** a	b	c	d
15. a	b	c	d	**30.** a	b	c	d	**45.** a	b	c	d

ANSWER SHEET, PART II

Name: _____

Instructions: Darken your answer to each question. Only one answer is correct. Recommend use of pencil. To delete an answer, cross through with an X.

1. a b c d	**16.** a b c d	**31.** a b c d	
2. a b c d	**17.** a b c d	**32.** a b c d	
3. a b c d	**18.** a b c d	**33.** a b c d	
4. a b c d	**19.** a b c d	**34.** a b c d	
5. a b c d	**20.** a b c d	**35.** a b c d	
6. a b c d	**21.** a b c d	**36.** a b c d	
7. a b c d	**22.** a b c d	**37.** a b c d	
8. a b c d	**23.** a b c d	**38.** a b c d	
9. a b c d	**24.** a b c d	**39.** a b c d	
10. a b c d	**25.** a b c d	**40.** a b c d	
11. a b c d	**26.** a b c d	**41.** a b c d	
12. a b c d	**27.** a b c d	**42.** a b c d	
13. a b c d	**28.** a b c d	**43.** a b c d	
14. a b c d	**29.** a b c d	**44.** a b c d	
15. a b c d	**30.** a b c d	**45.** a b c d	

ANSWER SHEET, PART III, PROBLEM A

FUNCTION POINT COUNT SUMMARY

Project Number _____   Project Name _____
Date of Count _____   Counter's Name _____

Instructions: Enter all function types included. For development and initial Function Point counts there will not be any entries in the Before columns. Annotate all function types added by the conversion. You may wish to use different sheets for files and transactions.

Description	Type	DETs	RETs/FTRs	Complexity	DETs	RETs/FTRs	Complexity
	ILF/EIF EI/EO/EQ	After	After	After	Before	Before	Before

ANSWER SHEET, PART III, PROBLEM B

FUNCTION POINT CALCULATION TABLE

Project Number B4U _____ **Project Name** Locator Application

Type of Count: (Development Project)/Application Count (circle one)

Phase of Count: (Proposal)/Requirements/Design/Code/Test/ Delivery (circle one)

Date of Count _____ **Counter's Name** _____

---

*Function Types	Low	Average	High	Total
External Inputs	×3	×4	×6	
External Outputs	×4	×5	×7	
External Inquiries	×3	×4	×6	
Internal Logical Files	×7	×10	×15	
External Interface Files	×5	×7	×10	

Total Unadjusted Function Points (UFPs) =

GENERAL SYSTEMS CHARACTERISTICS

Characteristic	Degree of Influence	Characteristic	Degree of Influence
1. Data Communication	4	8. On-line Update	3
2. Distributed Functions	0	9. Complex Processing	1
3. Performance	0	10. Reusability	3
4. Heavily Used Configuration	0	11. Installation Ease	1
5. Transaction Rate	0	12. Operational Ease	3
6. On-line Data Entry	5	13. Multiple Site	1
7. End User Efficiency	3	14. Facilitate Change	2

Total Degree of Influence =

Value Adjustment Factor (VAF) = .65 + (.01 × TDI) = _____

Final Function Point Count (FP) = UFP × VAF = _____

*Development Function Point Count includes function types added by the conversion. Application Function Point Count does not include conversion requirements. An application count after an enhancement must include all existing function types, including those unchanged.

ANSWER SHEET, PART III, PROBLEM C

FUNCTION POINT COUNT SUMMARY

Project Number _____   Project Name _____
Date of Count _____   Counter's Name _____

Instructions: Enter all function types included. For development and initial
Function Point counts there will not be any entries in the Before columns. Annotate all function types added by the conversion. You may wish to use different sheets for files and transactions.

Description	Type	DETs	RETs/FTRs	Complexity	DETs	RETs/FTRs	Complexity
	ILF/EIF EI/EO/EQ	After	After	After	Before	Before	Before

APPENDIX

CFPS PRACTICE
EXAMINATION ANSWERS

ANSWER SHEET, PART I

Name: David Garmus

Instructions: Darken your answer to each question. Only one answer is correct. Recommend use of pencil. To delete answer, cross through with an X.

1. a b c **d**	**16.** a b c **d**	**31.** a b **c** d
2. a b c **d**	**17.** a b c **d**	**32.** a b c **d**
3. a b c **d**	**18.** a b c **d**	**33.** a **b** c d
4. **a** b c d	**19.** **a** b c d	**34.** a b c **d**
5. a b c **d**	**20.** a b **c** d	**35.** a b c **d**
6. a b c **d**	**21.** **a** b c d	**36.** **a** b c d
7. **a** b c d	**22.** a **b** c d	**37.** **a** b c d
8. a **b** c d	**23.** a b **c** d	**38.** a b **c** d
9. a **b** c d	**24.** a **b** c d	**39.** a **b** c d
10. a b c **d**	**25.** a **b** c d	**40.** a b c **d**
11. a b **c** d	**26.** a b **c** d	**41.** a b c **d**
12. **a** b c d	**27.** a b c **d**	**42.** a b **c** d
13. **a** b c d	**28.** a **b** c d	**43.** a b c **d**
14. a b c **d**	**29.** a **b** c d	**44.** a **b** c d
15. a b c **d**	**30.** a **b** c d	**45.** a b **c** d

ANSWER SHEET, PART II

Name: David Garmus

Instructions: Darken your answer to each question. Only one answer is correct. Recommend use of pencil. To delete answer, cross through with an X.

1. a b ⓒ d	**16.** a ⓑ c d	**31.** a b c ⓓ
2. a ⓑ c d	**17.** ⓐ b c d	**32.** a ⓑ c d
3. a b ⓒ d	**18.** a b ⓒ d	**33.** a ⓑ c d
4. a ⓑ c d	**19.** a b c ⓓ	**34.** a ⓑ c d
5. ⓐ b c d	**20.** a ⓑ c d	**35.** a ⓑ c d
6. a b c ⓓ	**21.** ⓐ b c d	**36.** a b ⓒ d
7. a b c ⓓ	**22.** ⓐ b c d	**37.** a b ⓒ d
8. a b c ⓓ	**23.** a ⓑ c d	**38.** ⓐ b c d
9. a ⓑ c d	**24.** a b ⓒ d	**39.** a ⓑ c d
10. a b ⓒ d	**25.** a b c ⓓ	**40.** a ⓑ c d
11. a b ⓒ d	**26.** a b c ⓓ	**41.** ⓐ b c d
12. a b ⓒ d	**27.** ⓐ b c d	**42.** ⓐ b c d
13. ⓐ b c d	**28.** a b c ⓓ	**43.** a b ⓒ d
14. a ⓑ c d	**29.** a b c ⓓ	**44.** a ⓑ c d
15. a b c ⓓ	**30.** a b c ⓓ	**45.** a ⓑ c d

ANSWER SHEET, PART III, PROBLEM A

FUNCTION POINT COUNT SUMMARY

Project Number _____   Project Name _____
Date of Count _____   Counter's Name _____

Instructions: Enter all function types included. For development and initial Function Point counts there will not be any entries in the Before columns. Annotate all function types added by the conversion. You may wish to use different sheets for files and transactions.

Description	Type	DETs	RETs/FTRs	Complexity	DETs	RETs/FTRs	Complexity
	ILF/EIF EI/EO/EQ	After	After	After	Before	Before	Before
Company Contact Data	ILF	12	1	L			
Notes Data	ILF	4	1	L			
Error File	EIF	4	1	L			
Create Contact	EI	12	2	A			
Update Contact	EI	12	2	A			
Delete Contact	EI	4	2	L			
Packet Sent	EI	5	2	A			
Phone Contact	EI	6	3	H			
Notes Retrieved	EQ	4	1	L			
Retrieve Contact	EQ	12	1	L (output side)			

ANSWER SHEET, PART III, PROBLEM B

FUNCTION POINT CALCULATION TABLE

Project Number B4U_____   Project Name Locator Application

Type of Count: (Development Project)/Application Count (circle one)

Phase of Count: (Proposal)/Requirements/Design/Code/Test/ Delivery (circle one)

Date of Count _____   Counter's Name _____

*Function Types	Low	Average	High	Total
External Inputs	1×3	3×4	1×6	21
External Outputs	$\times 4$	$\times 5$	$\times 7$	0
External Inquiries	2×3	$\times 4$	$\times 6$	6
Internal Logical Files	2×7	$\times 10$	$\times 15$	14
External Interface Files	1×5	$\times 7$	$\times 10$	5

Total Unadjusted Function Points (UFPs) = 46

GENERAL SYSTEMS CHARACTERISTICS

Characteristic	Degree of Influence	Characteristic	Degree of Influence
1. Data Communication	4	8. On-line Update	3
2. Distributed Functions	0	9. Complex Processing	1
3. Performance	0	10. Reusability	3
4. Heavily Used Configuration	0	11. Installation Ease	1
5. Transaction Rate	0	12. Operational Ease	3
6. On-line Data Entry	5	13. Multiple Site	1
7. End User Efficiency	3	14. Facilitate Change	2

Total Degree of Influence = 26

Value Adjustment Factor (VAF) = .65 + (.01 × TDI) = .91

Final Function Point Count (FP) = UFP × VAF = 42

*Development Function Point Count includes function types added by the conversion. Application Function Point Count does not include conversion requirements. An application count after an enhancement must include all existing function types, including those unchanged.

ANSWER SHEET, PART III, PROBLEM C

FUNCTION POINT COUNT SUMMARY

Project Number _____   **Project Name** _____
Date of Count _____   **Counter's Name** _____

Instructions: Enter all function types included. For development and initial
Function Point counts there will not be any entries in the Before columns. Annotate all function types added by the conversion. You may wish to use different sheets for files and transactions.

Description	Type	DETs	RETs/FTRs	Complexity	DETs	RETs/FTRs	Complexity
	ILF/EIF EI/EO/EQ	After	After	After	Before	Before	Before
Field Help	EQ	<5	1	L			
Field Help	EIF	<5	1	L			
Screen Help	EQ	<5	1	L			
Screen Help	EIF	<5	1	L			
Overdue Contact Report	EO	6	1	L			

VENDOR LISTING

VENDOR LISTING

Vendor	Product Name	Functionality							
		Time	Defect	FP Reposit	FP Calculate	Estimate	Process Assess	Measure Reposit.	Import/Export
AGS Management 1060 First Avenue King of Prussia, PA 19462	FirstCASE					x	x		
Angel Group 1012 Meadow Creek Drive Las Colinas, TX 75038	FP Mentor				x				
Applied Business Technology 316 Broadway New York, New York 10013	Metrics Manager	x		x					x
	Project Workbench								x
	Project Bridge								x
Computer Associates 2 Executive Drive Fort Lee, NJ 07024	CA Metrics								x
	CA-FPXpert				x	x			x
	CA-PLANMACS							x	x
	CA-ESTIMACS	x				x			x
DDB Software 217 West Union St. Ashland, MA 01721	S.M.A.R.T. Counter			x	x				x
	S.M.A.R.T. Tracker		x		x				x
	S.M.A.R.T. Predictor					x			x
	S.M.A.R.T. Risk						x	x	
	S.M.A.R.T. Data							x	
Galorath Associates, Inc,. P.O. Box 90579 Los Angeles, CA 90009	SEER-SEM					x	x		
Martin Marietta Price Systems 300 Route 38 Moorestown, NJ 08057	PRICE-S					x			x
MSB2 344 W. Bonniwell Rd Mequon, WI 53097	FPSII			x	x			x	x

212

VENDOR LISTING

Vendor	Product Name	Functionality							
		Time	Defect	FP Reposit	FP Calculate	Estimate	Process Assess	Measure Reposit.	Import/Export
Protellicess Services 429 Santa Monica Blvd #460 Santa Monica, CA 90401	Micro Man Esti-Mate	x	x			x			x
Primavera Systems Two Bala Plaza Bala Cynwyd, PA 19004	Project Planner					x			
Productivity Management Group 178 Foxhunt Lane East Amherst, NY 14051	Productivity Manager	x		x				x	
Quantitative Software Management 2000 Corporate Ridge Suite 900 McLean, VA 22102	SLIM	x				x			x
	PADS	x	x						x
	SLIM-Control						x	x	x
	Size Planner			x					x
Software Productivity Research 1 New England Exec Park Burlington, MA 01803	CHECKPOINT		x	x	x	x	x	x	x
	FP Workbench				x				

G

GUN COMPUTING SYSTEM FP COUNT—JUNE 1994

Updated GCS Function Point count performed in preparation for cost estimates for the NSFS Gun Enhancement for GCS. Updated count to cover: OS, DMS, HSMST, Coord Illum, and other enhancements made since Aug 92 update. These counts relate to the U.S. Navy Success Story in Chapter 11.

GCC FUNCTION POINT COUNT

GCC External Interfaces

1) C&D (Aegis Command & Decision System)
2) SPY (Aegis SPY-1D Radar System)
3) ACTS (Aegis Virtual Spare Computer)
4) GMP (Gun Mount Processor)
5) Gun Console UYQ-21 (Operator console)
6) Real-Time Monitor Terminal (Maintainence/Debug)
7) USH-26 Tape Drives (Data Extraction)

USH-26 Tape Drive

1) Tape Status Interrupt Word   1 EI L
2) Data Records   1 EO H

Real-Time Monitor Terminal Interface

1) Read Options   4 EQ L
2) Change Options   4 EI L
3) Command Responses   1 EO L
4) Misc Options   3 EQ L   2 EI L   2 EO L

Spy (Aegis SPY-1D Radar System) Interface

1) SPY Track Data Message
    ⇨ Gyro Indicator   1 EI L
    ⇨ Target Data, Track Mode, Sim Ind   1 EI H
2) AN/SPY-1D Tactical Status Message
    ⇨ Transmitter Status   1 EI L
3) Track Acquisition Request Message   1 EO A
4) Track Data Request Message   1 EO A
5) AN/SPY-1D Battleshort Order Message   1 EO L

C&D (Aegis Command & Decision System) Interface

1) C&D Track Data Message
    ⇨ Target/Track Data   1 EI A
        ⇨ Category   1 EI L
2) GCS Firing Int Alert Message   1 EI L
3) GCS Doctrine Message   1 EI A
4) GCS Engagement Order Message
    ⇨ Order (BE, ENG, CF, HF, ASSIGN)   1 EI H
    ⇨ Situation Doctrine   1 EI L
5) Ships Data Message
    ⇨ Ship Data   1 EI L
      Lat, heading, mag var, ownship
      speed, ownship N/E speed, curr
      set, drift
6) CGTN Reassignment Message
    ⇨ Target Data (CTSL, CGTN, GTN)   1 EI A
7) Console Assignment Message   1 EI L
8) Console Status Message   1 EO L
9) Shore Target Location Message   1 EO H
10) GCS Firing Status Message   1 EO L
11) Engagement Order Response Message   1 EO H
12) GWS Engagement Status Message   1 EO H

13) GWS System Status Message   1 EO H
14) Track Acquisition Message   1 EO A

GMP (Gun Mount Processor) Interface

1) Message 100—Initialization
   ⮑ Interface Status Data   1 EI L
   ⮑ Met, Spot, Ammo, Ballistics   1 EI H
2) Message 101—4 Hz Tactical Data
   ⮑ Ballistics/Ammo/Spot Data   1 EI A
   ⮑ Target Data   1 EI L
   ⮑ Ship Data   1 EI L
   ⮑ Gun Orders Data   1 EI L
      ⮑ HSMST Target Data /Radii   1 EI A
3) Message 103—Calibration Data   1 EI L
4) Message 310—SDC Interface Data   1 EI A
5) Message 311—DCP Interface Data   1 EI A
6) Message 312—Velocimeter Interface   1 EI L
7) Message 313—GDC Interface Data   1 EI L
8) Message 314—Clock Interface Data   1 EI L
   Message—DMS Interface Data   1 EI L
   Message—OS Interface Data   1 EI L
9) Message 104—4 Hz Tactical Data   1 EO H
10) Message 105—16 Hz Tactical Data   1 EO H

Gun Console UYQ-21—Operator Displays & Controls

1) DDI Operator Display Screens
   ⮑ MNT/Ball DDI Data Screen   1 EQ H
   ⮑ Other 3 DDI Data Screens   3 EQ L
   ⮑ Close Control Data   1 EQ A
2) DDI Common Outputs
   ⮑ Alerts   1 EO A
   ⮑ System Data Area   1 EO L
   ⮑ Tape Drive Status   1 EO L
   ⮑ System Faults   1 EO L
3) BDU Operator Display Screens
   ⮑ Doctrine/Type Select   1 EQ L   4 EI L
   ⮑ Status Screen   1 EQ L   13 EI L
   ⮑ Tactical (Graphics/Spots)   2 EQ H   3 EI A
   ⮑ Tactical/Target Centered   1 EQ H
   ⮑ Manual Inputs Screen   1 EQ A   1 EI A
   ⮑ Ship Navigation Screen   1 EQ A   1 EI A
   ⮑ NGFS Target Data Screens   1 EQ H   1 EI A

⇝ Coord Illumination Screen	1 EQ A	1 EI L	
⇝ Tape Test Screen	1 EQ L	1 EI L	
⇝ Target Generator Screen	1 EQ L	1 EI L	
⇝ Interface Monitor Screen	1 EQ L	1 EI L	
⇝ Sensor Select Screen	1 EQ A	1 EI L	

HSMST Operator Display Additions (New FPs)

⇝ Tactical (Page Selection)	1 EQ H		
⇝ HSMST Page (Target Type)		1 EI L	
⇝ HSMST Page (HSMST On/Off)		1 EI H	
⇝ HSMST Display			1 EO A
⇝ HSMST Page (Selection)	1 EQ A		

4) BDU Outputs Independent of Screens

| ⇝ Warnings | | | 1 EO H |
| ⇝ Minimum/Nominal/Maximum Entry Prompt | | | 1 EO A |

5) CCAEP Button Inputs

⇝ Firing Control Buttons		1 EI L	
⇝ Drop Track		1 EI L	
⇝ Tape Start /Stop		1 EI L	
⇝ Stow/Safe/Gun Control		1 EI L	
⇝ Counter Battery		1 EI L	

GCC Internal Data Groups

1) A RTM Debug/Memory File
2) H Smooth Target Track Data File—Surface, AA, Nav/Ref Sensor Tracks
3) L Gun Orders File (2Hz/32Hz, Stable/Deck, posn/stow/etc)
4) L Clock Time File
5) A Ammo Data /Inventory File
6) H Data Retrieval File
7) A Ballistics Data /Inputs
8) L Link Enable/Disable Status File
9) L Mode File (AA, SDF, NGFS & submodes)
10) L Ship Information File (course, speed, heading, roll, pitch, . . .)
11) L Ship Characteristics File (cutout zones, parallax, . . .)
12) L Projectile Track Data File (used for Calibration & Projectile Impact Algorithms)
13) H NGFS Target /Ownship Data File
14) L Engage Orders/Firing Authority/Doctrine File
15) L Console Assignment File
16) L HSMST Parameters File

Grand Totals of Function Point Components

	Total	Low	Avg	High
External Inputs	69	52	13	4
External Outputs	23	9	6	8
External Inquiries	27	15	6	6
Internal Logical Files	16	10	3	3

14 Complexity Factors

1)	Data Communications	5
2)	Distributed Data Processing	4
3)	Performance	5
4)	Heavily Used Configuration	4
5)	Transaction Rate	5
6)	On-Line Data Entry	5
7)	End User Efficiency	4
8)	On-Line Update	4
9)	Complex Processing	5
10)	Reuseability	1
11)	Installation Ease	1
12)	Operational Ease	4
13)	Multiple Site Use	2
14)	Facilitate Change	3
	Total	52

Adjustment Factor = 0.65 + (0.01*52) = 1.17

GCC Function Point Count

Components	Low Count		Average Count		High Count	
External Inputs	52×3	156	13×4	52	4×6	24
External Outputs	9×4	36	6×5	30	8×7	56
External Inquiries	15×3	45	6×4	24	6×6	36
Int Logical Files	10×7	70	3×10	30	3×15	45
Subtotals		307		136		161

Total Unadjusted Function Point Count: 604

Value Adjustment Factor: 1.17

Function Point Total: 707

GMP FUNCTION POINT COUNT

GMP External Interfaces

1) Fore GDC
2) Aft GDC
3) Master Clock
4) Slave Clock
5) SDC/Gun Mount
6) Velocimeter
7) GCC (Gun Console Computer)
8) Gun Mount Control Panel (Operator console)
9) Real-Time Monitor Terminal (Maintainence/Debug)
10) USH26 Tape Drive (Test I/O only)
11) DMS—Data Multiplex System
12) Optical Sight

GDC Interface—Input Only

1) Ship Attitude (Role, Pitch, Heading)/Time Tag and status/data valid	1 EI L

Clock Interface—Input Only

1) Time word at 1024Hz & Data Valid EXF	1EI L

Real-Time Monitor Terminal Interface

1) Read Options	4 EQ L		
2) Change Options		4 EI L	
3) Command Responses			1 EO L
4) Misc Options	3 EQ L	2 EI L	2 EO L

Velocimeter Interface

1) Command Responses	1 EI L	
2) Initial Velocity Measurement	1 EI L	
3) Velocimeter Commands		1 EO L

Optical Sight Interface

1) Disable communications	1 EI L	
2) Position/Status message	1 EI L	
3) Orders/Ownship Data message		1 EO L
4) ACT Sync message		1 EO L
5) Initiate/Terminate communications		1 EO L

DMS Interface

1)	Status Msg	1 EI L
2)	16Hz Attitude Msg	1 EI L
3)	4Hz Navigation Msg	1 EI H

GCC (Gun Console Computer) Interface

1)	Message 104—4 Hz Tactical Data		
	⇨ Target Data	1 EI L	
	⇨ NGFS Data	1 EI L	
	⇨ Ship Data	1 EI L	
	⇨ Ballistics Data	1 EI A	
	⇨ Control Data	1 EI A	
2)	Message 105—16 Hz Tactical Data		
	⇨ Control Data	1 EI L	
	⇨ Error Recorder Data	1 EI L	
3)	Message 100—Initialization		1 EO H
4)	Message 101—4 Hz Tactical Data		1 EO H
5)	Message 102—16 Hz Tactical Data		1 EO H
6)	Message 103—Calibration Data		1 EO L
7)	Message 310—SDC Interface Data		1 EO A
8)	Message 311—DCP Interface Data		1 EO A
9)	Message 312—Velocimeter Interface Data		1 EO L
10)	Message 313—GDC Interface Data		1 EO L
11)	Message 314—Clock Interface Data		1 EO L
12)	Message—DMS Interface Data		1 EO L
13)	Message—Optical Sight Interface Data		1 EO L

SDC/Gun Mount Interface

1)	Parellel Output Data		
	⇨ Gun/Fuze position & rate orders		1 EO L
	⇨ Alerts		1 EO L
	⇨ Tests		2 EO L
2)	SDC Input Channel Numbers		1 EO L
3)	Serial Output Data		
	⇨ Status msgs		1 EO L
	⇨ Guided projectile		1 EO L
	⇨ Laser/Seeker codes		1 EO L
	⇨ Charge/Fuze/Proj orders		1 EO L
4)	Serial Fuze Data Callup		1 EO L
5)	Gun Position	1 EI L	
6)	Serial Input Data	1 EI L	
7)	Guided Proj	1 EI L	

8) Seeker/Laser   1 EI L
9) Ammo Inventory Slot   1 EI L
    ↪ Proj Code/Ammo/Charge/Fuze/Count

USH-26 Tape Drive

1) Tape Status Interrupt Word   1 EI L
2) Test Records   1 EO A

Gun Mount Control Panel—Operator Displays & Controls

1) Outputs Independent of Screens
    ↪ Alerts/Warnings   7 EO L
    ↪ Min/Nom/Max Entry Prompt   1 EO A
2) Count of Operator Display Screens

	EQ	EI	EO
↪ PPI/Tactical	1 EQ H	4 EI A	
↪ Target Data /Tactical	1 EQ H		
↪ Ammo Manual Inputs	1 EQ A	4 EI A	
↪ Ballistics Manual Inputs	1 EQ L	3 EI A	
↪ Drum Inventory	1 EQ L	1 EI L	
↪ Link Status	1 EQ L	6 EI L	
↪ General Status	1 EQ A		
↪ NGFS/GDR Inputs	1 EQ L	4 EI L	
↪ NGFS/RDR Inputs	1 EQ L	1 EI L	
↪ Mode Control Screen	1 EQ L	4 EI L	
↪ GMP Display Test		1 EI L	1 EO L
↪ Gun Mount Tests	5 EQ L	5 EI L	5 EO L
↪ OS Drive Tests	2 EQ L	2 EI L	2 EO L
↪ Fuze Setter Tests	2 EQ L	2 EI L	2 EO L
↪ EAT Test Screens		9 EI L	7 EO L
↪ Tape Test Screens		2 EI L	2 EO L
↪ Interface Monitor Screens	5 EQ L	5 EI L	
↪ Target Generator	1 EQ L	1 EI L	
↪ Zero Ballistics	1 EQ L	2 EI L	
↪ Error Recorder	1 EQ L	3 EI L	
↪ Status Box Fields	1 EQ L		

GMP Internal Data Groups

1) A   RTM Debug/Memory File
2) L   Target Track File
3) L   Gun Orders File (2Hz/32Hz, Stable/Deck, posn/stow/etc)
4) L   Clock Time File
5) A   Ammo Data /Inventory File
6) H   Data Retrieval File

7) A   Ballistics Data/Inputs
8) L   Link Enable/Disable Status File
9) L   Mode File (AA, SDF, NGFS & submodes)
10) L   Ship Information File (course, speed, heading, roll, pitch, . . .)
11) L   Ship Characteristics File (cutout zones, parallax, . . .)
12) L   Error Recorder Function Code File
13) L   NGFS Target /Ownship Data File
14) L   Engage Orders/Firing Authority/Doctrine File
15) A   HSMST Parameters File

Grand Totals of Function Point Components

	Total	Low	Avg	High
External Inputs	87	73	13	1
External Outputs	56	49	4	3
External Inquiries	35	31	2	2
Internal Logical Files	15	10	4	1

14 Complexity Factors

1)	Data Communications	5
2)	Distributed Data Processing	4
3)	Performance	5
4)	Heavily Used Configuration	4
5)	Transaction Rate	5
6)	On-Line Data Entry	5
7)	End User Efficiency	4
8)	On-Line Update	4
9)	Complex Processing	5
10)	Reuseability	1
11)	Installation Ease	1
12)	Operational Ease	4
13)	Multiple Site Use	2
14)	Facilitate Change	3
	Total	52

Adjustment Factor = $0.65 + (0.01*52) = 1.17$

GMP Function Point Count

Components	Low Count	Average Count	High Count
External Inputs	73×3 219	13×4 52	1×6 6
External Outputs	49×4 196	4×5 20	3×7 21
External Inquiries	31×3 93	2×4 8	2×6 12
Int Logical Files	10×7 70	4×10 40	1×15 15
Subtotals:	578	120	54

Total Unadjusted Function Point Count: 752

Value Adjustment Factor: 1.17

Function Point Total: 880

BIBLIOGRAPHY

Albrecht, A.J., "Measuring Application Development Productivity," Proceedings of Joint SHARE, GUIDE, and IBM Application Development Symposium, October 1979, pp. 83–92.

Boehm, Barry W., *Software Engineering Economics*, Prentice-Hall, Englewood Cliffs, NJ, 1981, 767 pages.

Coad, Peter, and Yourdon, Ed, *Object-Oriented Analysis*, Prentice-Hall, Englewood Cliffs, NJ, 1991, 233 pages.

Crosby, Phil, *Quality is Free: The Art of Making Quality Certain*, McGraw-Hill, New York, NY, 1979.

Curtis, Bill, *Human Factors in Software Development*, IEEE Press, Washington, DC, 1986, 730 pages.

DeMarco, Tom, and Lister, Timothy, *Peopleware,* Dorset House, New York, NY, 1987, 188 pages.

Dreger, J. Brian, *Function Point Analysis*, Prentice-Hall, Englewood Cliffs, NJ, 1989, 185 pages.

Florian, Ken, "How to Use Function Points to Build a Contract", International Function Point User Group, Westerville, OH, Spring 1994 Proceedings.

Garmus, Dave, "Function Point Counting", *Software Development*, September 1993, pp. 67–69.

Garmus, Dave, *CACI Function Point Counting Manual*, CACI, Mechanicsburg, PA, 1989.

Garmus, Dave, *Huron Function Point Counting Guide*, Amdahl, Sunnyvale, CA, 1992.

Garmus, Dave, and Paskey, Walter, "Use of Software Metrics Within CACI Information System Development Projects", CACI, Arlington, VA, 1991.

Garmus, David (ed), *IFPUG Counting Practices Manual, Release 3.4*, International Function Point Users Group, Westerville, OH, July 1992, 78 pages.

Garmus, David, and Herron, David, *Function Point Analysis, A Guide to Sizing Software*, The David Consulting Group, Orange Park, FL, 1994, 197 pages.

Garmus, Dave, *Function Point Analysis for New Technologies*, The David Consulting Group, Orange Park, FL, 1994.

Garmus, Dave, *Certified Function Point Specialist Examination Training*, The David Consulting Group, Orange Park, FL, 1994.

Goodwin, Paul, "Comparing Mark II with IFPUG Function Points", International Function Point User Group, Westerville, OH, Fall 1994 Proceedings.

Herron, David, *Software Risk Assessment and Management*, The David Consulting Group, Framingham, MA, 1994.

Herron, David, *Taking the Risk Out of Software Management*, The David Consulting Group, Framingham, MA, 1994.

Herron, David, "Proposal for Ratio Based Function Point Calculations", Software Productivity Research, Burlington, MA, April, 1990.

Hetzel, William, *Making Software Measurement Work: Building an Effective Program*, QED Publishing, Wellesley, MA, 1993, 290 pages.

Humphrey, W.S., *Managing the Software Process*, Reading, MA, Addison-Wesley, 1989, 489 pages.

IBM, "AD/M Productivity Measurement and Estimate Validation", IBM Corporate Information Systems and Administration, IBM Corp., Purchase, NY, May 1984.

IFPUG, *Counting Practices Manual, Release 4.0*, International Function Point Users Group, Westerville, OH, January 1994, 294 pages.

Jones, Capers, *Applied Software Measurement*, McGraw-Hill, New York, 1991, 493 pages.

Jones, Capers, *Programming Productivity*, McGraw-Hill, New York, NY, 1986, 280 pages.

Jones, Capers, *Assessment and Control of Software Risks*, Prentice-Hall, Englewood Cliffs, NJ, 1994, 619 pages.

Jones, Capers, "A Short History of Function Points and Feature Points", Software Productivity Research, Inc., Burlington, Mass., June 1986, 65 pages.

Kemerer, Chris F., "An Empirical Validation of Software Cost Estimation Models, Communications of the ACM 30", May 1987.

Kemerer, Chris F., "Reliability of Function Points Measurement: A Field Experiment", Massachusetts Institute of Technology, Boston, MA, December 1990.

Keyes, Jessica, *Software Engineering Productivity Handbook*, McGraw-Hill, New York, NY, 1993, 651 pages.

Lusher, Paul W., *Productivity Baseline Report for MK-160 Gun Computing System Software*

Development, Gun Fire Control Systems Branch, Naval Surface Warfare Center, Dahlgren, VA, October 1991.

Lusher, Paul W., *Software Metrics and Development, Productivity for the MK-160 Gun Computer System*, Weapons System Department, Naval Surface Warfare Center, Dahlgren, VA, December 1991.

Lusher, Paul W., "Function Point Analysis for Real-Time Weapons Control", Weapons System Department, Naval Surface Warfare Center, Dahlgren, VA.

Putman, Lawrence, and Myers, Ware, *Measures for Excellence: Reliable Software In Time, Within Budget*, Prentice-Hall, Englewood Cliffs, NJ, 1992, 378 pages.

Rubin, H., *Software Engineer's Benchmark Handbook*, Applied Computer Research, 1992.

Symons, Charles, "Function Point Analysis-Difficulties and Improvements," *IEEE Transactions on Software Engineering*, January 1988, vol. 14, no. 1, pp. 2–11.

Symons, C.R., *Software Sizing and Estimating: Mark II Function Point Analysis*, John Wiley, 1991.

Yourdon, Edward, *Decline and Fall of the American Programmer*, Prentice-Hall, Englewood Cliffs, NJ, 1992.

Whitmire, Scott A., "An Introduction to 3D Function Points, Software Development", April 1995.

INDEX

The David Consulting Group

Function Point Counting Guidelines

INTERNAL LOGICAL FILE (ILF):

User identifiable group of logically related data or control information maintained within the boundary of the application
* logical, or user identifiable, data that fulfills specific user requirements
* maintained within the application
* modified, or maintained, through an elementary process
* not counted as an EIF for the application being counted

EXTERNAL INTERFACE FILE (EIF):

User identifiable group of logically related data or control information referenced by the application, but maintained within the boundary of another application
* logical, or user identifiable, data that fulfills specific user requirements
* referenced by, and external to, the application being counted
* not maintained by the application being counted
* counted as an ILF by another application
* not counted as an ILF for the application being counted

EXTERNAL INPUT (EI):

Processes data or control information that comes from outside the application's boundary and stands alone as an elementary process.
    Processed data maintains one or more ILFs, and is received from outside the application boundary

* maintains data in an ILF through an elementary process of the application
* smallest unit of activity meaningful to the end user in the business
* self-contained and leaves the business of the application in a consistent state
* for the identified process:
    - processing logic is unique from other external inputs for the application, or
    - data elements identified are different from other external inputs for the application

Processed control information may or may not maintain an ILF, and is received from outside the application boundary
* specified by the user to ensure compliance with business function requirements
* for the identified process:
    - processing logic is unique from other external inputs for the application, or
    - data elements identified are different from other external inputs for the application

EXTERNAL OUTPUT (EO):

Elementary process that generates data or control information sent outside the application's boundary
* sends data or control information external to the application's boundary
* sent through an elementary process of the application

* smallest unit of activity meaningful to the end user in the business
* self-contained and leaves the business of the application in a consistent state
* for the identified process:
  – processing logic is unique from other external outputs for the application, or
  – data elements identified are different from other external outputs for the application

EXTERNAL INQUIRY (EQ):

Elementary process made up of an input-output combination that results in data retrieval; the output side contains no derived data; no internal logical file (ILF) is maintained during processing
* input request enters the application boundary
* output results exit the application boundary
* data is retrieved and does not contain derived data
* input request and output results together make up a process that is the smallest unit of activity that is meaningful to the end user in the business
* self-contained and leaves the business of the application in a consistent state
* processing does not update an ILF
* for the identified process:
  – processing logic on the input or output side is unique from other external inquiries in the application, or
  – data elements making up the input or output side are different from other external inquiries in the application

FUNCTION POINT COUNTING
Count Weights

Type	Low	Avg	High	Total
EI	___x3 +	___x4 +	___x6 =	____
EO	___x4 +	___x5 +	___x7 =	____
EQ	___x3 +	___x4 +	___x6 =	____
ILF	___x7 +	___x10 +	___x15 =	____
EIF	___x5 +	___x7 +	___x10 =	____

FILE COMPLEXITY MATRIX

RETs	1-19 DETs	20-50 DETs	51+ DETs
1	Low	Low	Avg
2-5	Low	Avg	High
6+	Avg	High	High

INPUT COMPLEXITY MATRIX

FTRs	1-4 DETs	5-15 DETs	16+ DETs
0-1	Low	Low	Avg
2	Low	Avg	High
3+	Avg	High	High

OUTPUT COMPLEXITY MATRIX

FTRs	1-5 DETs	6-19 DETs	20+ DETs
0-1	Low	Low	Avg
2-3	Low	Avg	High
4+	Avg	High	High

GENERAL SYSTEM CHARACTERISTICS

If none of the guideline descriptions fit the application exactly, a judgment must be made about which Degree of Influence most closely applies to the application. These questions are answered using Degrees of Influence (DI) on a scale of zero to five.

0 Not present, or no influence
1 Incidental influence
2 Moderate influence
3 Average influence
4 Significant influence
5 Strong influence throughout

1. DATA COMMUNICATION

The data and control information used in the application are sent or received over communication facilities. Terminals connected locally to the control unit are considered to use communication facilities. Protocol is a set of conventions which permit the transfer or exchange of information between two systems or devices. All data communication links require some type of protocol. Score as:

0 Application is pure batch processing or a stand alone PC.
1 Application is batch but has remote data entry or remote printing.
2 Application is batch but has remote data entry and remote printing.
3 On-line data collection or TP (teleprocessing) front end to a batch process or query system.
4 More than a front-end, but the application supports only one type of TP communications protocol.
5 More than a front-end, but the application supports more than one type of TP communications protocol.

2. DISTRIBUTED DATA PROCESSING

Distributed data or processing functions are a characteristic of the application within the application boundary. Score as:

0 Application does not aid the transfer of data or processing function between components of the system.
1 Application prepares data for end user processing on another component of the system such as PC spreadsheets and PC DBMS.
2 Data is prepared for transfer, transferred, and processed on another component of the system (not for end user processing).
3 Distributed processing and data transfer are on-line and in one direction only.
4 Distributed processing and data transfer are on-line and in both directions.
5 Processing functions are dynamically performed on the most appropriate component of the system.

3. PERFORMANCE

Application performance objectives, stated or approved by the user, in either response or throughput, influenced (or will influence) the design, development, installation, and support of the application. Score as:

0 No special performance requirements were stated by the user.
1 Performance and design requirements were stated and reviewed but no special actions were required.
2 Response time or throughput is critical during peak hours. No special design for CPU utilization was required. Processing deadline is for the next business day.
3 Response time or throughput is critical during all business hours. No special design for CPU utilization was required. Processing deadline requirements with interfacing systems are constraining.
4 Stated user performance requirements are stringent enough to require performance analysis tasks in the design phase.
5 In addition, performance analysis tools were used in the design, development, and/or implementation phases to meet the stated user performance requirements.

4. HEAVILY USED CONFIGURATION

A heavily used operational configuration, requiring special design considerations, is a characteristic of the application (for example, the user wants to run the application on existing or committed equipment that will be heavily used). Score as:

0 No explicit or implicit operational restrictions.
1 Operational restrictions do exist, but are less restrictive than a typical application. No special effect is needed to meet the restrictions.
2 Some security or timing considerations.
3 Specific processor requirement for a specific piece of the application.
4 Stated operation restrictions require special constraints on the application in the central processor or a dedicated processor.
5 In addition, there are special constraints on the application in the distributed components of the system.

5. TRANSACTION RATE

The transaction rate is high, and it influenced the design, development, installation, and support of the application. Score as:

0 No peak transaction period anticipated.
1 Peak transaction period (e.g., monthly, quarterly, seasonally, annually) anticipated.
2 Weekly peak transaction period anticipated.
3 Daily peak transaction period anticipated.
4 High transaction rate(s) stated by the user in the application requirements or service level agreements are high enough to require performance analysis tasks in the design phase.
5 High transaction rate(s) stated by the user in the application requirements or service level agreements are high enough to require performance analysis tasks and, in addition, require the use of performance analysis tools in the design, development, and/or installation phases.

6. ON-LINE DATA ENTRY

On-line data entry and control functions are provided in the application. Score as:

0 All transactions are processed in batch mode.
1 1% to 7% of transactions are interactive data entry.
2 8% to 15% of transactions are interactive data entry.

3 16% to 23% of transactions are interactive data entry.
4 24% to 30% of transactions are interactive data entry.
5 Over 30% of transactions are interactive data entry.

7. END-USER EFFICIENCY

The on-line functions provided emphasize a design for end-user efficiency. They include:

* Navigational aids (e.g., function keys, jumps, dynamically generated menus)
* Menus
* On-line help/documentation
* Automated cursor movement
* Scrolling
* Remote printing (via on line transactions)
* Pre-assigned function keys
* Submission of batch jobs from on-line transactions
* Cursor selection of screen data
* Heavy use of reverse video, highlighting, colors, underlining, and other indicators
* Hard copy user documentation of on-line transactions
* Mouse interface
* Pop-up windows
* As few screens as possible to accomplish a business function
* Bilingual support (supports two languages; count as four items)
* Multi-lingual support (supports more than two languages; count as six items)

Score as:
0 None of the above.
1 One to three of the above.
2 Four to five of the above.
3 Six or more of the above but there are no specific user requirements related to efficiency.
4 Six or more of the above and stated requirements for end-user efficiency are strong enough to require design tasks for human factors to be included (for example, minimize key strokes, maximize defaults, use of templates, etc.).
5 Six or more of the above and stated requirement for end user efficiency are strong enough to require use of special tools and processes in order to demonstrate that the objectives have been achieved.

8. ON-LINE UPDATE

The application provides on-line update for the Internal Logical Files. Score as:
0 None.
1 On-line update of one to three control files. Volume of updating is low, and recovery is easy.
2 On-line update of four or more control files. Volume of updating is low, and recovery is easy.
3 On-line update of major Internal Logical Files.
4 In addition, protection against data loss is essential and has been specially designed and programmed in the system.
5 In addition, high volumes bring cost considerations into the recovery process Highly automated recovery procedures with minimum of operator intervention.

9. COMPLEX PROCESSING

Complex processing is a characteristic of the application. Categories are:

* Sensitive control (for example, special audit processing) and/or application specific security processing
* Extensive logical processing
* Extensive mathematical processing
* Much exception processing resulting in incomplete transactions that must be processed again (for example, incomplete ATM transactions caused by TP interruption, missing data values, or failed edits).
* Complex processing to handle multiple input/output possibilities (for example, multi-media, device independence).

Score as:
0 None of the above.
1 Any one of the above.
2 Any two of the above.
3 Any three of the above.
4 Any four of the above.
5 All five of the above.

10. REUSABILITY

The application and the code in the application, have been specifically designed, developed, and supported to be usable in other applications. Score as:
0 No reusable code.
1 Reusable code is used within the application.

2 Less than 10% of the application considered more than one user's needs.

3 10% or more of the application considered more than one user's needs.

4 The application was specifically packaged and/or documented to ease re-use, and application is customized by user at source code level.

5 The application was specifically packaged and/or documented to case re-use, and application is customized to use by means of user parameter maintenance.

11. INSTALLATION EASE
Conversion and installation ease are characteristics of the application. A conversion and installation plan and/or conversion tools were provided and tested during the system test phase. Score as:

0 No special considerations were stated by user, and no special set-up required for installation.

1 No special considerations were stated by user, but special set-up required for installation.

2 Conversion and installation requirements were stated by the user, and conversion and installation guides were provided and tested. The impact of conversion on the project is not considered to be important.

3 Conversion and installation requirements were stated by the user, and conversion and installation guides were provided and tested. The impact of conversion on the project is considered to be important.

4 In addition to (2), automated conversion and installation tools were provided and tested.

5 In addition to (3), automated conversion and installation tools were provided and tested.

12. OPERATIONAL EASE
Operational ease is characteristic of the application. Effective start-up, back-up, and recovery procedures were provided and tested during the system test phase. The application minimizes the need for manual activities, such as tape mounts, paper handling, and direct on-location manual intervention. Score as:

0 No special operational consideration other than the normal back-up procedures were stated by the user.

1-4 Select the following items that apply to the application. Each item has a point value of one, except as noted otherwise.
  - Effective start-up, back-up, and recovery processes were provided but operator intervention is required.
  - Effective start-up, back-up, and recovery processes were provided but no operator intervention is required (count as two items).
  - The application minimizes the need for tape mounts.
  - The application minimizes the need for paper handling.

5 Application is designed for unattended operation. Unattended operation means no operator intervention is required tooperate the system other than to start up or shut down the application. Automatic error recovery is a feature of the application.

13. MULTIPLE SITES
The application has been specifically designed, developed, and supported to be installed at multiple sites for multiple organizations. Score as:

0 No user requirement to consider the needs of more than one user/installation site.

1 Needs of multiple sites were considered in the design, and the application is designed to operate only under identical hardware and software environments.

2 Needs of multiple sites were considered in the design, and the application is designed to operate only under similar hardware and/or software environments.

3 Needs of multiple sites were considered in the design, and the application is designed to operate under different hardware and/or software environments.

4 Documentation and support plan are provided and tested to support the application at multiple sites, and application is as described by (1) or (2).

5 Documentation and support plan are provided and tested to support the application at multiple sites, and application is as described by (3).

14. FACILITATE CHANGE
The application has been specifically designed, developed, and supported to facilitate change. Examples are:

* Flexible query/report capability is provided.
* Business control data is grouped in tables maintainable by the user.

Score as:

0   No special user requirement to design the application to minimize or facilitate change.

1-5 Select which of the following items apply to the application.

   – Flexible query/report facility is provided that can handle simple requests; for example, and/or logic applied to only one Internal Logical File (count as one item).

   – Flexible query/report facility is provided that can handle requests of average complexity; for example and/or logic applied to more than one Internal Logical File (count as two items).

   – Flexible query/report facility is provided that can handle complex requests; for example, and/or logic combinations on one or more Internal Logical Files (count as three items).

   – Control data is kept in tables that are maintained by the user with on-line interactive processes, but changes take effect only on the next business day.

   – Control data is kept in tables that are maintained by the user with on-line interactive processes, and the changes take effect immediately (count as two items).

The David Consulting Group

David Garmus (904) 269–0211
David Herron (508) 881–1144